Penguin Education

A Sociological Portrait

Edited by Paul Barker

A Sociological Portrait

Edited by Paul Barker

A series from New Society

Penguin Books

Penguin Books Ltd, Harmondsworth,
Middlesex, England
Penguin Books Inc., 7110 Ambassador Road,
Baltimore, Md 21207, USA
Penguin Books Australia Ltd,
Ringwood, Victoria, Australia

First published 1972
Copyright © New Society 1972
This selection copyright © New Society 1972
Introduction and notes copyright © New Society 1972

Made and printed in Great Britain by
C. Nicholls & Company Ltd.
Set in Linotype Pilgrim

Contents

I would like to acknowledge the help I got from conversations with John H. Goldthorpe, Professor Peter Hall, Professor R. E. Pahl and Professor John Rex.

Paul Barker

Paul Barker

Introduction

This book takes a number of important sociological variables, and relates them to individuals. Hence, the title, *A Sociological Portrait*. Many of the variables are the standard preliminary categories of any survey – sex, occupation, marital status. Others are more oblique – associates, religion, politics. In each case, the authors have tried to pin down what a particular variable is a key to: what it tells us about a person. The intention has been to combine data with argument.

In a way this book stands sociology on its head. Sociology is, principally, about societies as wholes or about groups within society. But the purpose of this book is to ask what difference certain attributes make to an *individual*. If you know x about a person (age, say, or address, or sex), what else follows? And, just as important, what else does *not* follow?

Some sociologists may say that their work ought not to be used in this way. But there is no doubt that, whatever sociologists may prefer, the world does, in everyday life, set a lot of store by such attributes as are tackled in this volume and expects certain other things to follow from them. There must have been many people, filling in those standard questions at the start of a survey-form (they are known technically as 'face sheet variables'), who must have wondered what about themselves they were 'giving away' by their answers.

This volume first saw light as a series of articles in *New Society* but I always saw it as the subject-matter for a book. The authors, therefore, wrote with this in mind; and, though all were given the opportunity to make revisions for republication, not a great many have been made.

All the authors were asked to include as much *information* as they could so that, if nothing else, the series of pieces would be a useful, plain guide to the latest state of knowledge in various fields of sociology. I hope that many readers will use it in that way. Authors were asked to concentrate on material of direct relevance to Britain; but other material has not been ignored, of course, especially American. Some material crops up more than once, in different contexts; but that seemed to be part of the point, and such overlaps have, in general, been left in.

There are, of course, value-judgments involved in the choice of the variables included here. Thus, despite the novelty of including it in a series of this kind, and despite its relative neglect by academics, it seemed to me that one should try to pin down what an individual's consumption tells us about him. The effect of friends and associates is not an obvious variable either, but I thought that here, too, was something often ignored, not enough researched: hence Professor Pahl's chapter. In the case of race, I felt that more light might be generated by seeing race as a special case of a wider subject: hence, Professor Julius Gould on 'Nationality and Ethnicity'. But the most striking thing, to many readers' eyes, may be an omission, rather than a commission. There is no article specifically on class.

Why not? Several answers to that question are given in the chapter headed, 'Some Conclusions', in which R. E. Pahl gives his own assessment of what has gone before, from a sociologist's point of view. But one of my own main motives in omitting it was a feeling that, in Britain particularly, far too much sociology is devoted to class (though race risks running it close) as if it were, firstly, the be-all subject, secondly, a unified subject. So this book is one small attempt to swim the other way. By the end of it a reader will have learned about various components of class: income, occupation, education, family background. How he decides to piece them together – indeed, *whether* he decides to – is up to him.

Not all the authors interpreted their brief in precisely the same way. Some have written more generally than others. These have often been those who have been trying to trap a rather elusive subject. (Nationality/ethnicity and friends/associates are examples). Beyond a certain point, I thought these differences should stand. Sociology is not homogeneous in its approaches and judgments; nor is this book.

One of the interesting things, to me, about the series is the overall conservatism (with a small C) of its message. Alan Little on 'Education', for example, should be required reading for anyone who has too rosy a concept of the ease with which one can use 'social engineering' as a way to change society radically. (Individual injustices may be set right, but that is a different point). This message is confirmed, perhaps, by the strength of the variables described here which one can in no sense choose: family is the most notable of these. Contrary to mass-media rumour, society changes slowly.

On the other hand, it is good to find that a recurring theme is: these may be the 'facts' but what do they mean? Individuals, like society itself, are hard to pin down in neat etymological categories. There are thirteen attributes discussed in this book. Every individual can be classed according to all of them. But, in William James's phrase (quoted by R. E. Pahl), he may choose, to some extent, from among these 'empirical selves'. How he *sees himself* matters; and, related to that, how others see him.

Moral and philosophical questions cannot be dodged in sociology. The psychiatrist, R. D. Laing, who crops up in two of the chapters, owes much of his power to his ability to moralize, to his concern with people as individuals, and to his ability to *write* (even aesthetics cannot be kept out). It may seem, at the end of a book which has deliberately included a fair amount of data – of what can be measured – that sociology is about much more than precise measurement; and perhaps not even centrally about that.

A book like this may begin to answer some fairly straightforward questions (is it true that income and voting habits are closely related?; are all sex differences explicable by environment?; how does your address affect your life-chances?). But if it raises many wider ones, that is how it should be.

The Variables

1 Frank Bechhofer
Income

On buses, in pubs, and around dinner tables, whenever people are discussing their fellow-men phrases like 'What does he do?', or 'How does he earn his money?', are commonplace. When we see someone spending money in a particularly lavish way we may comment that he 'must be earning a packet', but we do not often *ask* how much someone earns. Indeed, one of the more interesting things one can say about income is that estimates of other people's earnings are often wrong by very large margins. The poorer members of our society tend to imagine the better-off, or even the rich, as earning sums not all that dissimilar to their own earnings, and certainly well below the reality; the more affluent members are nearly always surprised when they learn how large a proportion of the population, in our highly stratified society, lives in poverty.

This brief discussion raises several of the themes I want to pursue. Why it is considered wrong, or indiscreet, or impolite to inquire about someone's earnings but not about his occupation is a tantalizing question which I shall not go into here (indeed, does anyone know the answer?); but one thing is fairly certain: in Britain at least, knowledge of someone's occupation is a far more useful piece of information from which to deduce other things about him than income is. And the main reason for this is that income is anything but perfectly associated with the class and status divisions which affect behaviour to so great an extent.

Now, this is not to say that one can deduce nothing from income. At the very bottom, and to some extent at the very top, of the income distribution, one can deduce quite a lot (as we shall see); but in the middle, where most people are to be found, it is a great deal harder. The extremes of the distribution yield more predictable behaviour, because these are cut-off points above and below which income correlates highly with class and status.

Why, then, is income so often collected as a 'face-sheet variable' in surveys – i.e. as a piece of preliminary standard information? This introduces another paradoxical element. Elizabeth Gittus (1969), in her chapter on income in a recent book concerned with comparability of data, advised that income should *never* be collected as a face-sheet variable, because of the difficulties inherent in collecting the data, if indeed one can be sure exactly what it is one is collecting.

It is quite possible that one of the reasons why income is not as useful a predictor as one might imagine, is that the difficulties of definition and data collection have inhibited research. Titmuss, in his celebrated attack on those who had argued that incomes had become more 'equal' between 1938 and 1958 (they almost certainly did not), suggested the 'command over resources over time' as a definition, and thus drew attention to the importance of many hidden sources of income which do not appear in the tax statistics (the main source of information), and to devices which spread resources over a family and over time without control of them ever being lost.

This raises several important points. To the man in the street, income probably means earnings from employment. But this ignores such things as income from capital, from social security benefits, from tax concessions or from 'moonlighting'; it ignores windfalls like legacies, rebates and realizable capital gains; it ignores 'fringe benefits'; and, perhaps most important, it ignores the size of the unit being considered. *Family* income is certainly more relevant if we are concerned with consumption patterns (say), and even a poor assessment of this would require that we not only ask our man in the pub, or on the bus, what *he* earns, but also what his wife and possibly his children earn.

Unfortunately, using family income as obtainable from the published statistics and some surveys appears to reduce the already rather poor association of individual income with class and status, and thus further reduces the predictive power of the variable. It is, of course, true that family 'income', as Titmuss describes it, would probably give an *increased* association but the data are simply not available; nor are they likely to be.

Some indication of the size of 'hidden' incomes can be given, however. For instance, figures quoted by Lydall, from 1966 estimates by Hay-MSL for managerial staff, suggest that fringe benefits, as a percentage of basic salary, rise steadily from 11·2 per cent at basic salary, £1050, through 16·5 per cent at £2850, to 31·1 per cent at £7000 and over. If we know someone is a manager (additional information which would also tell us a great deal more), we can deduce fairly safely that the more he earns as basic salary, the smaller a proportion that salary is of his total earnings.

Further, Meade in 1964 calculated that while 5 per cent of the population in 1959 owned 75 per cent of the property, they obtained no less than 92 per cent of the income from property. A recent estimate (by PEP) suggests that, in 1969, 1 per cent of the population owned 20 per cent of the personal wealth. This suggests that Meade's figures may well still be accurate. The amount of property owned, and the income derived from it, being highly associated with class, would probably be a better predictor of behaviour than income itself, at any rate for the relevant minority of the population.

Titmuss's emphasis on resources over time draws attention to another feature of income. He differentiates between 'the different income classes who receive their income on a different time basis – weekly, monthly, yearly or in respect of longer periods. The individuals who constitute these classes at different points in time have, in consequence ... different sets of attitudes, behaviour and propensities in relation to getting, spending and hoarding.' Another point should be made at this stage. Stability of income may be a more important variable than size itself. One of the crucial elements in the market situation of various groups is the security of employment they possess, and the generosity of provision if they lose their jobs.

Knowing someone's income in the sense of knowing the (usually naive) assessments of income which appear in the official statistics and in some surveys is not likely to take us much further in knowing anything about an individual. Possession of a certain income does not automatically place someone in a particular social class. The arguments about the so-called *embourgeoisement* of the working class are well-known. I shall simply confine myself here to saying that I have no reason to change an earlier statement in the study, *The Affluent Worker*, with which I was associated – that affluent workers retain 'important areas of common social experience which are still fairly distinctively working class; that specifically middle-class social norms are not widely followed nor middle-class life styles consciously emulated; and that assimilation into middle-class society is neither in progress nor, in the main, a desired objective.'

For my purpose here, the main implication of the *Affluent Worker* study is that knowledge of a particular level of income does *not* enable one to predict social class. The considerable overlap of incomes between the manual and the professional, managerial, technical, administrative

and teaching strata is best seen by a look at family incomes, as given in the Family Expenditure Survey for 1970. While it is true that only 12 per cent of the 'middle-class' households had incomes below £25 a week, as opposed to 24 per cent of the 'working class'; and 46 per cent as opposed to 16 per cent had incomes over £50 per week – it is nevertheless the case that 43 per cent of the 'middle-class' group, and 60 per cent of the 'working-class' group, had incomes between £25 and £50 a week. The mean ages of the household heads for the two groups were almost exactly the same, although it should be noted that the manual households had a very slightly larger household size. I shall return to the topic of low-income families later on, but it is worth mentioning here that the only major difference in the mean ages for each income group is to be found in those earning less than £10 per week. Here the heads of the manual households had an appreciably higher mean age than the heads of the 'middle-class' families.

The Family Expenditure Survey confirms that income yields some weak predictions at the extremes of the distribution. Incomes of £80 a week are achieved by 15 per cent of the 'middle-class' households and by a mere 2 per cent of the manual ones – and then only at the cost of much overtime, shift working, danger and deprivation. It is a safe but unexciting bet that the very high incomes are, on the whole, earned by male, professional, managerial and executive groups. But it is emphatically not true that the life-styles of these groups bear much resemblance to each other. Nor does income give much help in distinguishing subgroups. Though studies are few and far between, it seems highly likely that the middle class is as heterogeneous as the working class – probably more so. Income grouping does not provide a unifying factor.

Nor is income a good predictor of voting behaviour. Income is a considerably weaker predictor than class – particularly, again, in the middle ranges of income, where most people are to be found.

But surely income must tell one something useful in the areas where it most impinges, such as housing and consumption patterns? Alas, not really.

Alan F. Sillitoe, in his recent *Britain in Figures*, shows 'that in terms of gross income, families in privately rented unfurnished dwellings (average £1224 a year) were less favourably placed than those in council accommodation (£1331 a year). Next come those who have bought their own housing (£1482 a year), and best off were those still buying with the aid of a mortgage (£1835). No doubt many of those who have completed the purchase of their own housing are now retired and have lower incomes than when they were paying for their mortgage.' So, clearly, there is *some* suggestion that those owning or buying their houses have higher incomes. But income *alone* is still a poor predictor.

Using the 1970 Family Expenditure Survey we can look at extremes, and see that even among those households with incomes over £60 a week, 21 per cent were living in local authority unfurnished housing (68 per cent were owning or currently purchasing their houses); and among those with incomes between £10 and £20, not only were 37 per cent in local authority unfurnished housing but a surprising 35 per cent fell into the 'ownership' category. The data allow us, once again, to compare the 'middle-class' and the manual groups, albeit somewhat crudely. It is immediately clear from the table that income is a very poor predictor.

The *types* of housing owned, or being bought, by the lower income group no doubt differed sharply from the £60 a week households; so one almost certainly can say that the quality of houses being purchased is lower, or the houses are smaller, or the districts less 'desirable' for the lower

Table 1

Occupational group	Household weekly income	Percentage in LA unfurnished housing	Percentage owning or purchasing
'Middle class'	Over £60	5	88
'Middle class'	£10–£25	13	46
Manual	Over £60	45	40
Manual	Under £25	55	23

income groups. But class will enter into this also, and simply knowing the income group without some additional information enables us to say very little with certainty – particularly as income is differently distributed over the life cycle for different social classes.

This last is an important point. At a given income level, age and stage in the family cycle will affect behaviour possibly as much as income itself; and, as ever, the effect varies by social class. It is, by and large, a feature of the middle class that they are more skilled in stretching their income forward in time to cover their old age (see Titmuss) and that financial assistance to young families is greater (see Colin Bell's book *Middle Class Families*).

If we look directly at expenditure patterns, as given in the 1970 Family Expenditure Survey, we certainly find some highly predictable trends by income. The proportion of income spent on housing varies linearly from 20·9 per cent in the under £10 a week group to 10·9 per cent for those with £60-plus. The higher the income, the greater the expenditure, but the smaller the proportion of total income. Similarly with food – from 30·6 per cent for those households with incomes below £10 a week to 20·1 per cent for those with £80-plus.

But social class cuts across these patterns in a complex way. For instance, the 'middle-class' households with weekly incomes over £25 (88 per cent of the 'middle-class' households have such incomes) spend more per week on housing than any of the manual income groups except the small proportion (8 per cent) with household incomes over £60. The mean weekly expenditure on tobacco of the manual group is greater than that of *any* 'middle-class' group.

On turning to the extremes of the income distribution, we immediately come up against a difficulty. Given that it is not generally possible to earn very high incomes except in upper-middle-class occupations, and almost certainly impossible to do so consistently and steadily over long periods without some such occupation, it should be a matter of some ease to say quite a lot about these high-income earners. In fact, there are no studies of a group like this in Britain, apart from some slender and dated material on managers, and one very recent study of the same occupational group. No work exists on high-income groups as such. There are stereotypes of middle-class behaviour, widely held by sociologists as well as others, but little hard fact. It is likely that this group will tend to be Conservative in politics, to possess all the consumer goods associated with affluence, to send its children to the 'public' schools, to have a somewhat above average number of such children, to be highly educated if in the 'professional' group, to obtain higher education for their children, to own property and capital, and so on. But to the best of my knowledge we do not really know; and it is certainly time we did.

Predictably, however, we know a good deal more about the other end of the distribution; and while the emphasis in British sociology on the 'working class' may have been counter-productive, the recent emphasis on poverty is very necessary. For one thing, the skew of the distribution is such that the poor are a far bigger group than the rich. Sillitoe gives after-tax personal income figures for 1966–7, placing 3·3 per cent over £2000 a year and 18·7 per cent between £275 and £500. Nor is this all. There are a sizeable number below £275 who do not appear on the income tax returns from which the figures are derived.

The 1970 Family Expenditure Survey gives 9·8 per cent of *households* with incomes below £10 a week and a further 8·9 per cent between £10 and £15. These figures represent just under 4 per cent and nearly 6 per cent respectively of the *people* covered by the survey. A good deal has been written on the problems of defining poverty (see, for example, Peter Townsend) and it is clear that the concept of poverty as a fixed income level required for subsistence, is not sociologically adequate. Nevertheless, whatever criteria are used it is probable that between 5 and 15 per cent of the British population may be said to be living in poverty.

It is all too easy to predict a good deal about *this* group from their income. The old, no longer earning and with inadequate provision in the form of pensions and so on, form a large part. The other major group consists of those whose chief wage earner gains inadequate wages to support his family. The family may be a large one; but, in this context, even a family of three is likely to be 'too large'.

It is worth mentioning in this connection that the low-income households described in the previous paragraph are predominantly adult. In the sample as a whole 29 per cent of the persons covered are under sixteen years of age. In the households with incomes below £10 per week, 6 per cent of the people involved are under sixteen; in the households in the £10 to £15 range, 14 per cent are under sixteen.

Other groups are those effectively without a wage earner, because of death, unemployment or sickness.

These categories merge to some extent, of course, in the sense that families may move between them. Very low-paid workers are particularly prone to unemployment and sickness, for example. Several studies have observed living conditions, summed up graphically by Coates and Silburn (1970) for their sample, as follows: 'the low-paid are not evenly spread, a thin layer of underprivilege across the nation, but herded together into ghettoes in which they share not only low wages, but a dozen other social depriva-tions, from slum houses, meagre public services, squalid urban surroundings at the material level; to the accompany-ing moral sense that nothing can be done, that they are at the bottom of the pit.'

The fact that we can say a good deal about low-income families, if we know nothing more than that they have a low-income, brings us back to my earlier points. First, it should be stressed that, even in this group, variables such as age and position in the family-cycle will make a big dif-ference. Secondly, we must remember that 'income' is a more sophisticated variable than is generally realized. Most studies of poverty start from a population defined in terms of some community, some ecological boundary, and then investigate the number of people within that area living in poverty (however the researchers choose to con-ceptualize and measure it). In British society, strati-fication more or less guarantees that these are one-class communities. Whether one takes the view that these are separate underclasses (in Michael Harrington's phrase) with a definite 'culture of poverty', or (as I would) that extreme inequality of power produces and perpetuates such groups is irrelevant here. They are working-class com-munities and it is improbable that their members will be able to counter the low incomes of (for example) old age in the way a middle-class person usually can.

Not all people or all households with apparently low in-comes will be found 'in poverty', unless income is viewed in the complex way outlined by Titmuss. The middle class, by and large, are able to arrange their affairs so that they are to some extent protected against unemployment, sickness, the deprivations of old age and so on. The position is well summarized by Miller and Roby (in Townsend's *The Concept of Poverty*) where they write: 'not pauperism but inequality is the main issue within high-income industrial societies.' The really striking prediction one can make about families in poverty is that they are, even more than most working-class families, powerless. Union membership tends to be lower, political involvement, nationally or locally, minimal.

So we come full circle. Knowledge of someone's income alone does not enable us to predict much about him or her. To make much use of the information we would need to know how the income is earned, in what job, with what stability, and with what fringe benefits. And we would need to know the 'real' income, knowledge of which in most cases is highly improbable ... in the normal course of everyday life is almost inconceivable. If one knew that much about someone, one wouldn't need to make predictions from their income, one would know pretty well everything anyway.

2 S. R. Parker
Occupation

There is a risk that it will become an un-thought-through cliché that, for most people, their daily occupation is not a central interest in their lives. The meaning and interest is said to have gone out of work, the culture to offer an increasingly rich non-work life. And it is true that though physically damaging occupations have declined as machines have been moved in, these have been replaced by routine and boring occupations more than by stimulating and involving ones.

Yet even the most enthusiastic proponents of the idea that non-work life is central have to admit that the influence of occupation is still powerful. For example, it is, for most people, their main (if not only) contact with any kind of organization. And notwithstanding do-it-yourself, it is the chief technological aspect of their environment. Maybe most of us find it easy to 'forget' our occupation when we leave the workplace; but, despite that 'forgetting', its influence can still be seen in the rest of our lives. Psychologically, the job – even the hated job – means something to a man or to a woman. This is seen most clearly when he or she loses it through retirement or redundancy.

Of course, it is easy to slide from talking about occupation to talking about a job. A man can have no paid job and yet still be engaged in an absorbing and perhaps socially useful occupation. This is even more self-evidently true of a full-time wife and mother. A *job*, and the money it brings, will determine a person's standard of living. An *occupation* (which includes, and goes beyond a 'job'), and the development of personality and social relationships it brings, will determine his standard of *life*.

The term 'occupation' is, in fact, frequently related to two rather different sets of indicators. One of these consists of variables connected with the job itself: skills used, hours worked, whether there is a shift system, and so on. The other set of indicators is of the social position which the occupation makes possible – as measured on such scales as social class and socio-economic group. Quite often, too, this latter set of indicators is itself used to infer something about less easily measured attributes, such as style of life or cultural values. Being in a working-class or middle-class occupation can thus be seen – not necessarily correctly – as signalling a whole range of attitudes and behaviour patterns commonly thought to be 'typical' of people in that position.

In recent years, the sociology of occupations has made substantial progress. We know more than we did about how the miner's working life relates to his family life; about the motives that lead distant-water fishermen to 'live it up' when they are ashore; and about the ethos shared by occupational communities such as printers. Admittedly, we do not yet know enough about what makes one man's occupation an exciting, valued and personally-developing fulfilment, and another man's occupation a boring, frustrating and personally-stunting waste of time. Nonetheless, occupation is a key sociological variable; some would say *the* key variable. It gives a good many statistical and sociological clues to an individual's behaviour and attitudes. I shall consider these under a number of broad headings – material standards, personal characteristics, personal activities, and social activities.

To look at *material standards* is obviously, in a way, to turn on its head some of the material in the preceding chapter on 'income'. To what extent does occupation predict income (leaving aside, for the moment, occupations not linked to earning a living? There are several complicating factors here. Where experience and training are necessary, income tends to increase with age – as, for example, among professional people. Where physical strength and stamina are at a premium, income tends to decline at a fairly early age – as, for example, among labourers. Some occupations have established rates or scales of pay; so that if we know that a man is a bus driver, or a particular class of civil servant, we have a fairly good idea of his income, within reasonably narrow limits set by age, length of service, and area of employment. But other occupations, especially those in which the service rewarded is hard to find a substitute for, produce much more varied incomes. If we know that someone is an author or an actor we can have no idea, from that information alone, whether he gets a miniscule or munificent income. In particular, there is a certain amount of myth attached to the incomes of people in the entertainment occupations, in the wide sense of that term. Thus, Football League players are often supposed to earn vast sums of money. In fact, only the top 5 per cent earn over £7000 a year gross. About 70 per cent of all soccer players earn less than £3000, and most of them well below that. Furthermore, the average professional soccer player is earning only for about ten years. After this, he has to try his hand at some other occupation.

Expenditure is a function of income rather than of occupation. But occupation does play a large part in determining income. The Family Expenditure Survey lists the average expenditures of British households by very broad groups, according to the head of the household's occupation. The 1970 figures show that people in professional, technical, administrative, managerial and teaching occupations (average weekly income, £55) spent £41 on average each week. People in manual occupations (average income, £36) spent £29. It is notable how the lower-income earners, in both groups, managed to spend more than they earned — an indication that they had mortgaged the future.

But how does occupation affect *personal characteristics*? Take health, first of all. The type of work you do affects your health in many ways. Statistics covering manufacturing industries show that, if you are employed in the metal manufacture industry, your chances of having an accident at work are about nine times greater than if you are employed in the clothing and footwear industry. Occupation is also related to the incidence of certain diseases. Miners have a high rate of duodenal ulcer and farm workers a low rate; this reflects the different degree of anxiety besetting these occupations. Conductors of double-decker buses and postmen are less subject to coronary heart disease than the more sedentary drivers and clerks. The occupation of the father influences the health and survival chances of his children, too. Children of manual worker fathers have relatively high mortality rates from bronchitis, pneumonia, tuberculosis and congenital malformation.

One's occupation is associated with having characteristic attitudes, both to the job and (as I began by saying) more generally in non-work life. Attitudes appropriate to the kind of work arise even during training, or perhaps in the process of self-selection before training. Not only is occupation a major element in the self-identity of most males (and a good many females) in our society, but this process starts well before entering the world of work. American studies have shown how this 'identification with an occupation' develops among trainees. Prospective social workers tend to have 'people-oriented' values; business students are reward-oriented; and so on. In the occupational world itself, type of work, and frequency of contact with the employer, are associated with attitudes of militancy or conservatism. Generally speaking, if you know that someone is a non-manual employee, you will probably be right in predicting that he identifies to some extent with the middle class; and, if he is a member of any organization connected with work, it is likely, even nowadays, to be a staff association, rather than a trade union of the traditional kind.

With machines having been brought into offices, and 'staff status' given to increasing numbers of manual workers, however, the old distinctions based on occupational status are becoming blurred. But they have by no means disappeared. A few years ago, a sample of the British public was asked what sort of people they regarded as belonging to the middle and working classes: 61 per cent defined the middle class by their job, but 74 per cent defined the working class this way. Another important difference in attitudes is that typical of professional people, specialists and 'cosmopolitans' (to use Alvin Gouldner's term) on the one hand, and administrators, generalists and 'locals' on the other. The chances are that a professional person or specialist will attach more importance to his particular expertise, and less to his employing organization. An administrator or generalist will show a high loyalty to his organization, but be more transferable within it.

Type of occupation is a reasonably good predictor of job satisfaction. Research suggests that there are separate scales for manual and non-manual occupations. More satisfaction is found at the higher levels of skill in each group. American studies show that there are enormous occupational differences in the proportions of people who would try to get into a similar type of work, if they could start again: 93 per cent of university professors at one extreme, and 16 per cent of unskilled car workers at the other. If involvement in work is measured by such variables as being fully extended in the job, having work colleagues as close friends, and letting work encroach on leisure, then the occupations associated with high work involvement seem to be mainly service ones, concerned with the problems and development of people. The occupations associated with low work involvement are more often business or industrial ones, concerned with impersonal things, or concerned with personal relations only on a business basis.

A number of things must be grouped under the broad heading of *personal activities*. In the case of education, research makes it clear that the children of manual-worker fathers are at a disadvantage in gaining admission to grammar school and to university, and in achieving academic success generally. But the disadvantage (compared with children of middle-class families) is getting less: life-styles are tending to converge and old working-class prejudices against education are tending to diminish. But further education, which is often related to entry into, or advancement within, a professional occupation, seems likely, for some time, to have such groups as teachers and social workers heavily outnumbering most others.

The time available for leisure, the ways in which it is spent, and the functions it serves in the pattern of life, may all be traced to the type of work done. Trade unions have been successful in gradually reducing the standard working week of their members, even if the total hours worked have often been reinflated by overtime. But the equivalent has not been achieved by other employees. The extent of obligations connected with work – whether, for example, one finds it necessary to 'keep up' with the subject of one's work by spare-time reading – influences one's amount of leisure time. One survey has shown that bank workers have, on average, about an hour a day more leisure than child care or youth employment officers.

Greater involvement in work seems generally to be

matched by a more active leisure life. On the other hand, a more routine occupation is likely to provoke one of two reactions: spillover of the boredom of work into leisure, or explosive compensation in leisure for what is lacking in work. A further possibility is to separate work life and leisure life by assuming a permanent double identity. In that case, it is, by definition, not possible to discover what sort of a person a stranger is by asking only about his occupational background and position. It is equally important to ask about his other, non-work, identity.

The rates at which people change their jobs, or move their homes, are affected by their occupations. A worker in the construction or shipbuilding industry is likely to have many more jobs in his lifetime than someone of managerial or executive status. The idea of the career, as a progression of jobs with increasing responsibilities, rewards and status, is mostly confined to non-manual occupations. And even in some of these, it is more euphemism than reality. Another form of linkage of jobs – occupational inheritance, or sons following in their fathers' footsteps – is particularly noticeable among professional and high administrative employees, though it does happen in other occupational groups.

A tendency to move home (as opposed to jobs) with above-average frequency is related to being in a middle-class, and particularly professional, occupation. Hence the description, 'the migratory élite'. Until recently, it would also have been true to say that middle-class people travelled more often, and greater distances, from home than working-class people. But with package holidays the difference between occupational groups in this respect has almost certainly narrowed.

The relationship between suicide and occupation or class has been the subject of considerable study in both Britain and America. Some researchers have found that the wealthier sections of a city appear to have more suicides than the low-income neighbourhoods. Other findings point to a higher rate for white-collar and professional groups than for manual-worker groups. There are certainly differences in suicide rates within these broad occupational groups, which reflect particular types of work experience. Lonely occupations, such as domestic service and lodging-house keeping, have high rates. Occupations which bring men into close contact with each other, such as miners and the clergy (though there are reinforcing factors here!), have low rates. This strengthens Durkheim's classic explanation of differential rates of suicide in terms of the incidence of 'anomie' (or rootlessness) in a community.

In a very general sense, mobility may be said to account for many of the differences between occupational groups. This is most clearly seen in the more obvious forms, like changing jobs or moving home. But it also applies to movement away from traditional family patterns, differing activity in leisure life, and the extent of mixing with other people. This theme of mobility underlies many of the differences in *social activities*, in which the influence of occupation (often mediated by social class or status) can be seen. Styles of family living vary considerably between the traditional working class and the middle class, though there is some evidence of convergence in less traditional areas, like suburbs and new towns.

The isolation of the husband's occupational life from the wife's domestic life is breaking down, where new standards of 'affluence' require both husband and wife to work, and the husband consequently to share domestic tasks. But some particular occupational differences remain and are worth noting. According to census figures, the proportion of married people in certain occupations varies considerably. For example, among those in banking and bill-discounting it is 309 per 1000, while among those in market gardening it is 695 per 1000. Such differences reflect partly the age structure in different occupations, partly the age of marriage, and partly the propensity to marry (in the examples I have mentioned, the sex ratio is not an important factor, since each contains about one third of women). Thus, bank employees are below average in age, and it has in the past been expected of them that they will not marry too young. This, again, is probably changing.

Until a generation or so ago, it would have been true to say that fertility varied inversely with socio-economic status: the higher the status, the lower the fertility. Recent studies, however, suggest the reverse. Changing attitudes towards, and increasing opportunities for, women's employment outside the home have encouraged larger numbers of women in higher socio-economic groups to combine family life with a (possibly interrupted) career. Meanwhile, the wives of working class husbands, more aware now of the economic and social costs of having many children have shown an increasing tendency to plan small families – and they have been helped in this by the greater ease of female contraception. The care and rearing of children has been much researched in terms of alternating fashions of strictness and permissiveness in middle-class and working-class patterns. A more specific influence of occupation is its 'visibility' to children. A father whose workplace is adjacent to his home is likely to serve as a model to his children when they come to develop their own career. This is far less likely if the father follows a technically complex occupation which does not impinge on home life.

The propensity to belong to groups, clubs and associations of different kinds varies markedly with occupation. The general conclusion from a large number of studies is that the higher the socio-economic status, the greater the number of associational memberships, and the greater the likelihood of taking a leading or active part in them. Not only is the rate of membership different for the various socio-economic strata, but also the type of activities in those associations to which they belong. Professionals and managers are more likely to belong to civic associations, historical societies, country clubs and dining clubs; manual workers are more likely to belong to fraternal orders, patriotic groups and religious associations. The study of 'deviant' cases can be instructive. Thus, manual workers who were local government councillors were found to have a strong tendency to become more highly involved in their council work than those from other occupations, and the behaviour and general attitudes of these councillors was consistent with their regarding their public duties as a form of compensation for a paid job that did not use their potentialities.

It will be noticed that, in reviewing the ways in which occupation is a key variable in explaining the differences between people in many other respects, I have made much use of words like 'influences', 'relates to', 'is associated with' and 'predicts'. But all this does not add up to a kind of occupational determinism, according to which, if we know a man's occupation, we know many other *facts* about him. We are dealing, in all cases, not with perfect, one-to-one relationships, but with *probabilities*. We have, too, to beware of the intervening variable or third factor: *a* may relate to *b* only because both are caused by *c*. This is a point I made when talking about training: if we discover that social workers are willing to involve themselves much more in their occupations than most other employees, how much of this is due to the nature of the work they do and how much to the type of person attracted to that kind of work in the first place?

The mechanization of labour, and the consequent obsolescence of many occupational skills, has produced an increasing tendency for people to identify with their employing organization more than with the routinized set of operations they perform. It is easier, and somehow more acceptable, to say you work at Ford's or IBM than to say you are a roofing-felt trimmer or a key-punch operator. Not only is there a levelling of skills, but it is also less likely now than in the past that you can tell what a person does from his off-work appearance. Insofar as this is a reaction against the subordination of family, personal and cultural life to the needs of production, it is a healthy sign. To the extent that it signifies an occupational structure which provides many jobs that are best forgotten in terms of worthwhile human experience, it seems more questionable.

3 Derek Wright
Sex Differences

It seems that when groups of people are systematically marked off from each other by obvious physical characteristics, we immediately begin to infer that there will also be associated personality and behavioural differences. One of the most obvious facts about any person is his or her sex; and the biological fact of sex difference has given rise to more deeply held, and more stereotypic, conviction about correlated psychological differences than any other comparable physically-based classification of people, with the possible exception of race.

The mythology of sex differences is part of our culture; and, for all kinds of emotional and social reasons, people have an investment in maximizing or minimizing them. We even have an absurdity of some people believing that, in some total sense, one sex is innately 'superior' to the other. Convictions of this kind are seldom, if ever, rooted in evidence; the pattern seems to be that we are indoctrinated into the mythology first, and then interpret our experience of the other sex in its light. Hence, even if, for many people, research weighs little in the balance against personal belief, it is worth asking what the facts are, as existing research reveals them.

Turning to that research, we are at once faced with an embarrassingly large body of data. Numerous psychological experiments and sociological surveys have found the sexes to vary significantly on a wide diversity of behavioural measures. So far, no exhaustive catalogue of this material exists. But there are several excellent reviews of the more important, stable and consistent differences between the sexes. They allow us to make some generalizations which have a basis in fact. (Some of these reviews are listed in the 'Notes on Further Reading' at the end of the book.)

Before describing these differences, I must make certain qualifications. The bulk of the evidence comes from English-speaking countries, and in particular from the United States and Great Britain, though it is by no means confined to these. Then, it is important to realize that the differences I shall report represent *average* differences, or occasionally differences in *range* of behaviour. Though these differences are statistically greater than could be reasonably expected by chance, they are often small in magnitude. The point is an obvious one, but it is easily forgotten. Lastly, a more detailed assessment of the evidence than I can give here, would require a close scrutiny of the nature of the measuring instruments used in each study.

The psychological dimension which has received most attention in discussions of sex difference is probably intelligence. As many people have noted, genius and unusual creative originality in almost all aspects of life have been, hitherto, overwhelmingly male characteristics; among those who are acknowledged as having made important creative contributions in the arts, sciences, religion, industry, education and so on, men heavily outnumber women. Feminists sometimes claim that this is wholly due to the crippling handicap of the sex role imposed on women in nearly all cultures. But this argument is not entirely convincing. For there are areas where the handicap for women has been less great, such as literature, music and religion, in which women have been expected to be involved, yet in which their original contributions have still fallen far short of those of men. Furthermore there are many men of genius who faced handicaps of a different kind which seem equally daunting. Of course, it does not follow from this that women lack the innate ability for creative achievement; it may well be that they simply lack the temperament or motivation to realize their potentialities. Since many of the handicaps previously experienced by women are in process of disappearing, it will be interesting to see whether this difference between the sexes starts to disappear as well. At the other end of the scale, however, it is clear that among the severely mentally defective, males again predominate, and no one appears to have seriously questioned the genetic basis of this difference.

Studies of general IQ among large samples of the population have failed to find any consistent average differences between the sexes. This is not necessarily a particularly meaningful finding, however, because many tests of general intelligence are adjusted, during their construction, so as to eliminate or minimize sex differences. A more fruitful question is to ask whether there are divergences in specific abilities. Here the results do yield an interesting and fairly consistent pattern.

As far as tests of mathematical reasoning are concerned, there is, in general, little evidence of any difference between the sexes during childhood and early adolescence; but nearly every study has found that adult men do better at mathematical tests than adult women do. In spatial reasoning – i.e. the ability to think about forms and objects in space – the superiority of the male is much more clearcut at every age. The same can be said of tests of mechanical and scientific aptitude, and tests which involve 'breaking set'. In this last type of test, the subject is given an initial set or attitude which in fact impedes finding the solution to problems, so that what the test measures is a readiness to reorientate oneself and restructure the problem. It is interesting, too, that certain tests of 'field dependence', such as those requiring the subject to spot a shape which has been so embedded in a context that it has, so to speak, disappeared into it, also favour men. This suggests that males may tend to be more analytic, and that women are more impressionistic and influenced by immediate context.

It is in the area of verbal skills that the female's unequivocal superiority shows through. A great many studies confirm that girls speak earlier, have greater fluency and better articulation, wider vocabulary, utter longer and more grammatical sentences, read earlier and better, and are better at spelling. There are some signs that this advantage is, to some extent, lost by adulthood; and, in tests of verbal reasoning, the sexes do not differ consistently. One of the commonest beliefs about the sexes is that men are more logical than women. Studies using tests of abstract reasoning offer no support at all for this belief; females have been found to perform just as well as males. Tests of memory also fail to differentiate the sexes.

Whether the better-established divergences in cognitive functioning derive from sex-linked genetic effects specific to intelligence, or whether they are due to the different personality and motivational patterns between men and women, remains an open question. In any case the conceptual division into intelligence and personality obscures the fact that the two are essentially indivisible. Certainly there are many personality differences between the sexes, which could be offered at least as a partial explanation of the intellectual ones.

A finding of great consistency is that females of all ages display more interest in other people than males do. Even as young as six months, girls have been found, in controlled situations, to spend more time looking at faces. Recent studies of attachment behaviour, during the second year of life, suggest that girls are more 'person-oriented', and boys more 'thing-oriented'. At later ages, females are more interested in personal relationships, disclose more of themselves to others, know more about others, and remember names and faces better. Various tests indicate that women have a greater need for close, intimate relationships. At the same time, girls appear to be somewhat less motivated by the desire to compete with, and do better than, others. There is some evidence that they respond more empathically to the needs of others; and they more often enjoy and seek out situations in which they can nurture and care for others.

It is probable that this greater involvement with people underlies certain other findings. On measures of 'social desirability', girls are more inclined to describe themselves in a manner which they think others would approve. Studies of the effects of group pressure frequently show that females, with the exception of those in later life, are more conforming than males; they are more likely to give way and agree with the majority opinion. It has been observed that girls tend to keep more closely to the rules and conventions that are operating in any social situation. But the evidence does not, on the whole, suggest that they are more likely to resist the temptation to deviate when it seems improbable that anyone else will know. Indeed, it has been found that they are more inclined to lie when this appears the only way of giving a more favourable image of themselves to others. Much of the data on the moral behaviour of the sexes can be encompassed by the statement that girls do not have stronger consciences than boys, but they do have a greater need to maintain a good reputation with others.

One of the most universal facts about females is that they are less often found guilty of breaking the laws of society; and this is true at all age levels. Above all, they do not commit crimes of violence. The typical feminine offences are prostitution and petty theft. There are doubtless many reasons for this. The evidence shows that girls identify more closely with their families, and from an early age see themselves as eventually forming families of their own. They are also subjected to closer supervision and control from parents and other adults. They are, therefore, less likely to form delinquent gangs. Their greater concern for reputation plays a part in this. But one very important factor is that they are less inclined to physical aggression.

The evidence on this last point is striking. Quite a large number of studies, using a wide variety of measuring techniques, agree in finding girls less given to violence towards others, and they display rather more anxiety about taking part in physical aggression. The obvious explanation lies in the lesser muscular strength of women, and in the powerful influence of the prevailing social expectation that to be feminine is to be gentle, submissive and affectionate. Boys on the other hand are expected to be more aggressive and are often praised for being so. However, there are considerations which suggest that this may not be the whole explanation. Firstly, the sex difference in aggression has been found to exist from a very early age – i.e. before the age of two. Secondly, a comparable sex difference has been consistently found in a number of other species. And thirdly, aggressiveness in males has been clearly linked with male sex hormones, or androgens, in other species, and there are some clinical signs that a similar link may exist in men. It should be added, though, that several studies have indicated that, again from quite an early age, girls engage in more *verbal* aggression towards others than do boys.

Probably related to the question of aggression is that of social dominance. Far and away the most common family structure, throughout the world, invests the adult male with primary authority. It has even been asserted – for example, by Margaret Mead – that, in every known society, women have been subject to the authority of some male.

The general tendency for women to be more submissive,

conformist and concerned with other people, is reflected in the way that their beliefs and values deviate from those of men. For example, in a large-scale cross-cultural study, involving countries as varied as China, Japan, India and Norway, it was found that women stressed values related to sympathy for, and service of, others and submission to their needs, and were generally more concerned with conserving what had been achieved than with initiating change. Politically women tend to be more conservative, though they are markedly less interested in politics. In their expressed moral beliefs, women can be counted on to judge more things wrong, and judge them more wrong, than men – though there are signs that, in certain circumstances, women are more sympathetic towards wrongdoers. They are, also, of course, much more religious than men on the usual criteria of church-going and fervour of belief, though they have been singularly uncreative in this field and appear content to fill the role of dutiful and orthodox follower.

The differences I have listed have all been uncovered by research; and there are more, such as that women more often suffer from neurotic depression than men, and have been found to be more introverted on personality tests. But none of them offers many surprises to anyone conversant with the current stereotypes of the sexes. And it could be argued that the most impressive aspect of this research is not the average differences I have described – real and significant as these are – but the degree of overlap between the sexes. There are females who are more physically aggressive than many males, just as there are males who are more submissive and religious than many females. Nevertheless, these average differences exist; they are important; and they appear to be deep-rooted. What is their origin?

There are two points of view that are commonly adopted. The first attributes the differences primarily to innate, biological factors; and the other primarily to upbringing, to social pressures and to cultural expectations. Unhappily, research does not allow us to make any firm and unequivocal choice between them, for the biological distinction is invariably associated with different, and sometimes radically different, kinds of social experience. The individual always knows his own sex, and this knowledge will in itself condition his behaviour. At best, we can make some tentative inferences based on, for example, establishing that a form of behaviour is tied to some physiological process in which the sexes are known to vary, or showing that the behavioural divergence occurs so early in development that an explanation in terms of environment alone becomes less convincing.

There is the growing body of clinical data on those rare individuals whose sex is uncertain and intermediate. Such evidence can show how powerful the influence of assigned gender can be, and how early in development its effects are registered. But it does not help us understand the ways in which normal sex differentiation affects behaviour.

There is the evidence of the cross-cultural stability of sex differences; but, as evidence of genetic influence, this is much weakened by the fact that, though child-rearing practices vary widely across cultures, the basic differences in the way the sexes are treated vary little. It follows from all this that any conclusions we draw must have a large element of personal judgment and emphasis in them.

Since today the tendency seems to be to discount the effect of biological factors, it is as well to be clear what is involved in them. For my present purposes, there are five general points to be made.

First of all, from the genetic point of view, the sexes differ systematically to the extent of one chromosome, and this is a considerable difference. In his book *Genetics and Man* Professor C. D. Darlington goes so far as to assert, in agreement with earlier assessments, that 'the gravest consequence of the chromosome difference between the sexes is ... that we have to regard the two sexes as no less different genetically than two related species.'

Secondly, the differences in physiological structure and function, which follow from these genetic differences, progressively reveal themselves in a developmental sequence through life. It is in early adulthood, when women are conceiving and bearing children, that these differences are at their greatest. But the two major steps in this progression are at the fifth or sixth week after conception when, in the male foetus, the intervention of androgenic hormones ensures appropriate genital structures in an organism hitherto more accurately described as female; and at puberty when, in regard to androgen-estrogen balance, the sexes – up till then very similar – radically diverge. In the second half of life, there is a discernible tendency for the sexes to grow more similar to each other again.

Thirdly, the physiological differences are not confined directly to the reproductive function. To take some obvious examples, general rate of maturation is in many respects accelerated in girls; and, in the adult, muscle development, height, voice depth and susceptibility to certain diseases, are all greater in males. Less well-established are such findings as that women have a more marked physiological reaction to stress and recover more quickly; and their sense of smell is more acute.

Fourthly, it seems inconceivable that the many structural and functional differences will not have some behavioural consequences. But it is probable that most of these consequences will be indirect, and result from interaction with particular kinds of environment. To take a simple example, it seems likely that the lesser muscular strength of the female has contributed to the evolving of stringent prohibitions against male violence towards her, at least in some societies, and at the same time to the development in females of alternative ways of expressing aggression.

Lastly, there are certain qualifications to be made. Sexual differentiation of structure and function is a good deal less pronounced among human beings than it is in some other species; and within each sex there is wide variability to be found. In the case of a great many of those structural features which discriminate the sexes, there is, here again, some measure of overlap between them. And the vastly greater learning capacity found among human beings ensures that biological factors will be less important sources of differences in behaviour. Their influence will show itself, not in the simple determination of behaviour patterns, but rather through setting limits on the range of behaviour that can be acquired, and on the ease with which it is learned.

The area of response, which we might expect to be most closely connected with the primary biological function of sex differences, is sexual behaviour. The evidence suggests that the sexes do vary quite widely. Leaving aside those behavioural differences directly due to anatomical differentiation, there are two main ways in which the sexes tend to differ.

The first is that women are potentially capable of a more intense and prolonged sexual response than men. The evidence for this derives from the observations of Masters and Johnson (and others), who report that, in women, sexual arousal is more diffuse, and involves more widespread vasocongestion than in the male; and that women are capable of multiple orgasms. It also seems, however, that women vary more in their sexual response and that it is more closely tied to affection. Clinical observation has tended to emphasize the greater importance for women of more general emotional arousal in their sexual experience.

In contrast, the male sexual response is simpler, and more differentiated and isolated from other forms of autonomic arousal.

The second is that sexual drive, or motivation for specific genital experience, is in general less strong in women. This looks like the most reasonable construction to place on the convergence of a number of lines of research. Thus, surveys have found that women initiate sexual activity less frequently than men; that they can more easily tolerate sexual deprivation and even suppress sexual activity altogether; that they are more easily satisfied by sexual experience that falls short of orgasmic release; and that they are more likely to engage in sexual activity for motives other than sexual ones, such as for example to please their partners or to experience close bodily contact.

Whereas the factual differences seem clear enough, their explanation is more problematic. The current, popular view appears to be that the differences in sex drive can be attributed wholly to cultural pressures and consequent early conditioning. However, there are considerations which suggest they have a biological basis as well.

In the first place, there is the link between sex hormone secretion and sexual drive. Insofar as the two are related, it is clear from the evidence that it is the male sex hormones which relate to erotic interest in both sexes. However, the relationship is not a close one. A certain level of androgen in the blood stream seems a necessary condition for the emergence and maintenance of sexual motivation in both sexes; beyond this minimal level there can be wide variability in androgen secretion without the intensity of sexual motivation being much affected. But there is clearly a possibility (it is no more) that the considerably lower levels of androgen secretion in women are related to their apparently lower sexual drive.

The evidence relating hormones to erotic interest

strongly suggests that sexual motivation is to a very large extent acquired through learning, and that the brain is heavily implicated. To a considerable extent, sexual motivation is a function of such mental activities as remembering, anticipating and imagining on the one hand, and perceptual stimulation on the other. And, here again, there appear to be sex differences. Experiments with certain other species indicate that removal of parts of the brain diminishes male sex drive to a greater extent than that of the female. So far, no comparable evidence exists for men and women, but the animal studies suggest the possibility that, for them too, the brain is somewhat less involved in women. Then, interview surveys and experiments indicate that women are less susceptible to erotic stimuli of a visual kind, and are less aroused by literature describing sexual activity. It seems that they think less about sex and more about love. Finally, data, such as that provided by Kinsey on the relationship between age and sexual activity, could be construed as indicating that women acquire their sexual motivation more slowly and with more difficulty. And they are certainly less likely to learn abnormal forms of sexual behaviour.

Where does this leave the current habit of discounting the importance of biological factors in the production of these differences in sexual response? Certainly, no one can deny the massive effects of cultural conditioning. But it is difficult to study recent research on sexual behaviour without feeling that the existing differences have biological roots, which will continue to exert their influence when cultural expectations have changed.

It is hardly necessary to document the fact that the role expectations for the sexes are still widely different in our society. Studies confirm the point I have already made – that parents expect their sons to be less dependent and more achievement-orientated. Girls are expected to be more gentle and affectionate. But the really interesting point is the apparent tendency, nowadays, for these roles to become less clearly differentiated. There are obvious benefits from this greater flexibility in sex role. It increasingly enables the individual to work out the role that fits, rather than to adjust to a role already prescribed. It may well make for more fruitful relations between the sexes, by reducing the extent to which these are controlled by social expectation. And it may well make it possible for us, in the future, to discern more clearly the nature and extent of the influence on behaviour of the structural and physiological differences.

4 Geoffrey Hawthorn
Family Background

Although there is still (and must continue to be) much dispute about the relative importance of ties of kinship in industrial societies, there can be little doubt that the absolute importance of such ties, and especially the immediate ones, remains great. One's family of origin is still, by definition, the one institutional affiliation one cannot choose; it is an affiliation to an institution that for several years is virtually total; and it is an affiliation that is perhaps more difficult to renounce in later life than any other.

These are truisms. But so is the fact that all sociological findings are dubious. The methods by which observations are made are frequently crude and unreliable, and thus the generality, the realism and the precision of any finding is more often than not very much in doubt. This is as true of research into family background as of that into any other field, and indeed perhaps more so, for this is an area in which accurate observation of the crucial mechanisms is virtually impossible. It is therefore essential to be deeply sceptical of what follows. The first set of truisms encourages one in this post-Freudian climate to lay almost everything at the door of early upbringing, as the tendency of some studies in fields so apparently remote as political behaviour and economic growth reveals; but because of the force of the second set one must be constantly on guard. It may be that one's family remains with one, but with what force and for how long remain almost wholly uncertain.

An examination of the ways in which it might do so could take many forms, and this is not the place to discuss their various merits and demerits. I have thus somewhat

arbitrarily chosen to look first at certain correlations between family structure and the characteristics of children,
second, at the internal dynamics that might explain such
correlations; and third, and most briefly, at the variety of
social and economic situations in which families exist and
which might themselves, as antecedent factors, in turn explain some of these dynamics.

The most elementary structural variable of a family of
two parents and children is its size, which is to say the
number of children in it. Most of the British work on the
effects of family size for subsequent development has been
done in the longitudinal study being made by J. W. B.
Douglas and others of a 1946 birth cohort (or generation),
though much information has also come from James Nis-
bet and others. Unfortunately, as Oldman, Bytheway and
Horobin pointed out in 1971 in an article on 'Family
structure and educational achievement', associations between a child's characteristics and the number of its
brothers or sisters have been invoked by various people at
various times to support differing and sometimes incom-
patible hypotheses: at this point, therefore, I do not intend
that the results I mention shall be taken at anything more
than their face value.

Douglas, and Oldman and his colleagues, have both provided typical, and typically puzzling, sets of results. They
largely turn around observed differences in measured intelligence, and even if such measures do not reflect pure intelligence (whatever that may be), it is perfectly reasonable to
assume that they do reflect interesting and important differences of some kind. Douglas found that children's
measured IQ dropped as the number of brothers or sisters
increased, in all social classes though most severely in the
upper working class (the Registrar General's social class
III manual). Oldman and his colleagues generally confirmed this, although they found that children in the top

social class were not significantly affected. Indeed, when they reclassified their subjects according to whether or not the parents said that they were regular users of birth control (a proxy measure, one would have thought, of social class), they found that although some decline in IQ was evident in children from families not using birth control, children's IQ actually rose with family size in those that did, from a mean of 107 to a mean of 126 (admittedly, there were few individuals at the latter extreme). Douglas found that in both middle- and working-class families the mother's interest in and attitudes towards her children were less strong and less positive as the number of children increased. But as far as any (conventionally assumed) adverse effects on the children were concerned, these decreased rather than increased over time, as the children got older.

Size of family alone has not attracted all the attention among more purely structural variables. Many investigators have also looked at the correlates and consequences of a child's ordinal position in the family, and a few at the rate of family formation. Francis Galton's classic *English Men of Science*, where a birth order effect seems to have been first systematically noted, is like many recent studies in taking older children (his were in fact adults) as experimental subjects. There is sense in this, if D. C. McClelland is to be believed in his opinion that the critical period for socialization for achievement comes between the ages of six and eight. Virtually all of these studies report a positive association between both measured IQ and other less precise (though perhaps more meaningful) characteristics of ability and achievement and birth order. The earlier you come, the brighter you seem to be, especially where the whole family is above average.

In two-child families, the greatest difference occurs where the elder is a boy and the younger a girl. This is perhaps a compound effect of the elder child (especially if first-born) receiving the full force of the parents' anxieties and ambitions, and of parents requiring girls to be less assertive and less independent than boys. John and Elisabeth Newson noticed that younger children were treated more indulgently (regardless of sex) in Nottingham, although there is some suggestion from recent historical work that childrearing in the midlands may have been more strict in the past than elsewhere, and this contrast may not therefore be so marked elsewhere or at other times. The Cornell study of upbringing in the United States, the Federal German Republic and England has found that the English (at least in Surrey, where the sample was drawn) treated their male and female children exceptionally differently. Oldman, Bytheway and Horobin make some interesting suggestions about the nature and consequences of members being ascribed different roles in families of different sizes; but these so far remain speculative. Younger children, of course, are more likely to experience a broken home, and even if the home does not break, they may be affected by changes within a marriage over time that we as yet know virtually nothing about.

We know less about the consequences of various rates of family formation than we do about the correlates of birth order, although Douglas did find that school pupils from two-child families in which birth intervals were of between two and four years scored higher in all tests than those with either shorter or longer intervals. The recent trend away from longer birth intervals, and especially away from the phenomenon of the late child, as well as that away from very short ones, will make the population more uniform in this respect, always of course assuming that, perhaps like Oldman *et al*'s birth control practice, length of birth interval is not a spurious variable. Indeed, and quite apart from the danger of such interpretative pitfalls, to take these and other correlations between structural features of the family and characteristics of the children at face value is to remain unclear about the causal mechanisms involved; and for some understanding of these one must turn to the dynamics of relationships within the family.

At issue here are the relationship between the parents and between them singly and together and their children. Sociologists have been happy since Elizabeth Bott's small study in London to distinguish couples according to their 'role segregation': that is to say, according to whether, and if so in what ways and to what extent, they decide and do various things together. Our understanding of this phenomenon in British society, and thus our understanding of its effects (if any) on upbringing, is however rather poor. One suspects that working-class marriages are more generally segregated than middle-class ones. This certainly fits with Melvin Kohn's rather generalized stereotype (in fact derived from American experience) of the middle-class father being supportive, and thus supplementing the mother, and of the working-class father being more absent and more punitive, thus complementing her. But Hannah Gavron's research in Kentish Town, the Newsons' in Nottingham, and Toomey's in Rochester and Chatham, have all found the most involved fathers of all to be those in class III, the intermediate group. For Gavron and Toomey it was the manual fathers, and for the Newsons the non-manual ones. These couples also tended to be more socially isolated than most, and to have exceptionally high and strongly felt aspirations for their children.

We do not know if Kohn's vision accords with behaviour in the upper and upper-middle classes, but several pieces of work on the lower social classes, or on more traditional communities like those of miners, corroborate it for those groups. As Hilary Land for one, however, has emphasized, this does not necessarily mean that lower-class families are arenas of paternal anger, maternal strain and childish anguish. Except where the father is under severe strain, as perhaps in mining and fishing and so forth, these families are as happy as others, although the children are not 'successfully' trained for that middle-class achievement that is measured by most personality and intelligence tests. It is nevertheless the case that in these lower-class families the mother acts out the role characteristic of mothers in all classes to an extreme degree: that is to say, the role of the main agent of upbringing.

The point is reinforced by its converse. In the best study we have of the consequences of a broken home, made by Illsley and Thompson in Aberdeen (and concerning only female children), it turned out that the least marked differences followed from those situations in which only the father, but never the mother, left home or died. This specialization within the family seems to be a particular feature of differentiated, industrial societies, societies in which the husband is subject in his work to a rigid time discipline in an institution separated in all ways from his home. Laslett's partly speculative reconstructions of family life in pre-industrial communities (in his *The World We Have Lost*, and in his introduction to a new volume, which he has edited, *Household and Family in Past Time*), and Arensberg and Kimball's description of County Clare before the war in their *Family and Community in Ireland*, point up the contrasts within British society.

It is (to say the least) consistent with this view of the importance of the mother that there should turn out to be marked differences in children according to the influence and behaviour of the mother in the family. Ainsworth and Bell have shown that a very early maternal response to crying has a considerable effect on the child's imagination, alertness and independence, as well as on the quality of communication between it and the mother in later child-hood. In a famous and illuminating study, also made in the United States (and reprinted in A. H. Halsey *et al*, *Education, Economy and Society*), Strodbeck discovered an association between the mother's power and authority in the family, her 'achievement score values', and those of her children. This association may explain the one noticed by Floud, Halsey and Martin in *Social Class and Educational Opportunity*, by Jackson and Marsden in *Education and the Working Class*, and by Douglas (although apparently refuted in a recent re-analysis of the 1949 social mobility data) between high achievement and success in the child, again in middle-class terms, and having a mother of higher status than her husband.

But this may also be explained by, if it does not itself explain, the fact that this phenomenon occurs most frequently in class III, where high aspirations are the norm. The long-term consequences of maternal style for children have been suggested by another American study, made by Moss and Kagan, in which it was claimed that the consequences of maternal hostility and protectiveness persisted and indeed in some respects actually increased over time into the period beyond childhood.

All these processes and others of a similar kind are going to be affected by the power the mother has in the family with respect to the children, and there is some indication that English mothers have more power in this respect than those in Federal Germany and the United States. They certainly seemed to the Cornell investigators to stress assertiveness, aggression and achievement more than did mothers in the other two countries, although quite what inference one draws from this I am not sure.

Nevertheless, this maternal power might already be declining. In his essay in Erik Erikson's *Youth, Challenge and Change*, and elsewhere, Keniston talking about young

American radicals (in whom the disjunction is perhaps most acute), has said that the rate of social change in the United States is now so high that parents cannot pass on experience that their children will see as valid for their own lives; and several people have pointed out that in an increasingly plural society, the family is supported less and less from other institutions. It is interesting to speculate on the possible future effects of the tendency on the one hand of early upbringing to continue as it has always done, reinforcing in the child its parents' values, and the tendency on the other of more and more of these children coming to reject what they have been taught to see as social anachronism.

But such external pressures, coming from the outside society to impinge on the child and the adolescent, are beyond my scope here. What are not are the pressures which come to impinge on the parents and thus affect the way in which they are able or wish to treat their children. Such pressures are not easy to define, but if one takes merely the familiar set of attributes (each of which is discussed elsewhere in this volume), something may be said. The parents' education and the household income seem most crucial. No one has shown a consistent effect of mothers' working, and things like 'social class' and 'social status' are of course nothing more than (usually implicit) aggregations of separate dimensions like education and income.

More highly educated mothers, not surprisingly, are more likely to stimulate the child's verbal propensity at an early age, as the research by Dorothy Henderson and others at the London Institute of Education has shown, for example; and from what I have already said, it follows that they are more likely to make a difference than a highly-educated father. Not, it may be said, that we really understand what is going on when we use bland phrases like 'stimulate verbal propensity'. One American study revealed that highly educated parents tended to produce children with a higher formal intelligence score, but that creative children came from anywhere. The depressive effects of a low income, often associated with a thin educational background, are likely to remove the father still further from the upbringing of his child. It is clear from the interviews that Dennis Marsden did in 'Northborough' and 'Seastone' for his *Mothers Alone*, and that Land has done in London, that to have little money, perhaps 60 per cent of the norm for the group, disproportionately increases the strain on mothers, whether they be alone (as in Marsden's study) or living with the father. It also restricts the ability of the parents to provide those things, like outings and parties and places for their children to play with their friends, which must make some difference to the child's adaptation to the social world of its peers and in particular to its ability to learn normal rules of social intercourse.

There is much to suggest that the nature of the father's work affects the couple's marital organization (more so than their 'social network' which, following Bott, most sociologists have looked at in this respect). It is not easy to specify what it is about various kinds of work that does this. But apart from the obvious importance of the time the father spends at it and where he does it, whether he travels and how tired he gets, there are the more intangible factors of the extent to which he is in a work situation that draws him into a masculine culture at variance with domestic concerns, and of the ways in which what he does affects his self-identity and self-esteem. It is interesting too to speculate about the effect that the declining amount of occupational transmission from father to son may have had, and the concomitant process of the transfer of this and other functions to educational and occupational institutions. Again, one might conclude, industrialization has separated fathers from their children to a marked degree.

But work and the family have for long remained two quite separate sociological fields, and we know virtually nothing about their connections. As research by Robert and Rhona Rapoport, in their *Dual-Career Families*, suggests, these connections are close, complex and crucial, and are a very obvious field for further investigation. Although it does not deal directly with children, a forthcoming study of the relationships between family and work in the London area by Young and Willmott will doubtless stimulate much necessary debate about them. One thing might, however, be said from work that has been published. Many have noticed an association between the father's general frustration with his work and his involvement with the family: but the reported associations are contradictory. In the lower-middle and upper working classes, the frustration spurs him to demand achievement from his children (and, incidentally, to have fewer of them); in the lower working class, it does the reverse.

Perhaps the best general indication of the importance of extra-domestic factors can come from one example. In another study of Thompson and Illsley's, on family building in Aberdeen, they found that larger families tended also to be those in which the mother was brought up in class V (the unskilled working class), had four or more siblings, was illegitimate, of below average height and had a below average verbal test score; and in which the father too came from class V, had four or more siblings, was illegitimate, still worked in a class V occupation, had recently changed his employer and was away for long periods; and in which the first child (despite any advantages following from a high ordinal position) was also of below average height at five and had a below average IQ score.

This truly depressing combination of circumstances

shows very clearly that any study of upbringing that con-
centrates solely upon the internal dynamics of the family
will miss illuminating explanations of those dynamics,
more importantly, will also miss possible explanations of
differences arising from what on the face of it seem similar
sets of parents, and most importantly, to the extent that it
fails to take into account the force of the combination of
circumstances (as Stinchcombe has said, in an argument
against Jensen on race and IQ) will perhaps actually be led
to make false causal imputations.

I remarked earlier that the generality of many sociological findings is in doubt: do they apply to most places
and most times, or are they severely restricted? Until we
do comparative work, we cannot know (and can therefore
be all the more bold or all the more cautious in our hypotheses). But what is reasonably certain is that the knowledge, if it can be taken as such, that I have summarized
here is conditional. It applies only to households consist-
ing of married couples and their children in a highly urbanized and largely industrialized environment. It very probably
does not apply to households where other kin are regularly
present, and to truly rural areas. To see the width of the
disparity at the present time one only has to look, to take
but one example, at accounts of child-rearing in isolated,
highly inter-related and truly communal communities like
those of the Hutterites in North America. And although
our past may not have been as different from the present
as some myths suggest, we must still recognise that even if,
as Laslett insists, households were relatively small, the conditions of employment for a large proportion of the society
were very unlike those we have now.

One might go further, and maintain that not only are
these findings limited to nuclear households in urban, industrial societies, but that they are also limited to a few
decades in such a society. What of the more recent past,

and of the future? Of the first we know little, and for generations now dead shall probably never know very much.
Anderson's work on mid-nineteenth century Preston suggests
that family ties were close in the early stages of industrialization and the concomitant migration to the towns,
and most middle-class families, as many other studies have
mentioned, used servants for much of their childrearing.
In all cases, larger family sizes must have meant less interaction between the parents and each child. But what difference such factors may have made remains obscure. For
generations still living, however, interviews of the kind
that Paul and Thea Thompson are doing (trying to pin down
people's memories) will tell us a great deal which will be
invaluable.

For those yet to be born, we may speculate luxuriously,
always remembering that futures have been more like pasts
than people have either wished or feared. Goldthorpe and
Lockwood, in the *Affluent Worker*, and Young and Willmott are only the most recent of many sociologists who
have said that we are moving to a more home-centred,
'companionate' pattern of family life, no doubt in part
because an increasingly rational society (in the purely
technical sense) provides fewer and fewer satisfactions
of a wider sort. Correspondingly, the family perhaps
now bears a greater emotional load than it has ever done
before in most social groups. Nevertheless, even if work
and leisure begin to become more satisfying for more
people, and even if the emotional load produces more
stress of various kinds, the fact remains that the nuclear
family does seem to be the simplest conceivable structure
for doing what it has to do, and even if we do not know
very much about how it does it, which is what this essay
has been about, that must be a very powerful restraint on
change.

5 Colin Bell
Marital Status

It is extraordinarily difficult to disentangle causes from consequences. Take, for example, the supposed effects of marital status on women's achievement. In 1961, 11 per cent of all women aged 30–34 were unmarried; yet 27 per cent of all women doctors were unmarried. Of the really high achievers enshrined in the *Dictionary of National Biography*, only 10 per cent of those who died this century were unmarried; yet no less than 42 per cent of the women remained unmarried. It is rarely suggested that marriage hinders male achievement (though Cyril Connolly lists 'the pram in the hall' among the *Enemies of Promise*), but what can be made of the female evidence? Did these worthy women fail to marry because they were high achievers; or were they high achievers because they failed to marry? The answer to this question in the face of our present knowledge tends to depend more on our values and prejudices than on analysis.

We do know, however, that more and more people not only get married but (as the table on page 65 shows) have been, at any rate till recently, getting married sooner. The 'never-married' proportion of the British population dropped from 61 per cent in 1871, to 51 per cent by 1931 and was 41 per cent in 1961. Over these 70 years, usually between 3 and 5 per cent more men than women over 61 were single. Because of the different life expectations of the sexes, there are always more widows than widowers, about three times as many; and about 10 per cent of all women are widows. This difference between the sexes would be even greater if it were not for the different ages at which the sexes get married. Women marry younger; and though, since 1966, there has been a decline in the proportion of teenage marriages, nearly one in three of all girls still marry in their teens and one in ten of all men. The overall age of marriage has declined steadily this century, and it remains to be seen whether the trend towards fewer teenage marriages will continue. (If better contraception is a main cause, it may.) But there are no signs that fewer people are getting married. Spinsters, maiden aunts and unmarried mistresses have all declined in numbers. In 1911 nearly 20 per cent of women in their forties had never married. This had fallen to 8 per cent by 1968.

Table 1 *Age at marriage in Britain in this century* (% by age)

Spinster marriages	1901	1911	1921	1931	1951	1961	1966	1967	1968
16–19 years	8·4	7·6	9·2	10·1	16·8	28·4	32·6	30·1	29·0
20–24 years	47·6	47·1	47·8	47·2	53·2	51·2	51·5	54·5	56·2
25–29 years	27·8	29·9	27·6	28·3	17·9	11·7	9·3	9·1	9·1
30+	16·2	15·4	15·4	14·4	12·1	8·7	6·6	6·3	5·7
total	100	100	100	100	100	100	100	100	100
Total spinster marriages (in thousands)	268	286	326	326	358	350	382	382	402
Average age of spinsters marrying	25·6	25·6	25·5	25·5	24·6	23·3	22·7	22·7	22·7

Bachelor marriages	1901	1911	1921	1931	1951	1961	1966	1967	1968
16–19 years	1·6	1·6	2·1	2·0	2·8	7·0	10·2	9·7	9·3
20–24 years	40·4	37·5	38·0	36·5	45·6	52·8	56·3	58·4	60·0
25–29 years	35·0	38·0	35·6	40·5	31·8	25·6	21·8	20·8	20·3
30+	23·0	22·9	24·3	21·0	19·8	14·6	11·7	11·1	10·4
total	100	100	100	100	100	100	100	100	100
Total bachelor marriages (in thousands)	261	280	327	317	349	347	378	378	398
Average age of bachelors marrying	27·2	27·3	27·6	27·4	26·8	25·6	24·9	24·8	24·7

Source : adapted from *Social Trends,* vol 1, no. 1, table 13

As the age of marriage has declined, first pregnancies have come earlier. This implies, with increasing life-expectancy, that there will be many more four-generation families. At the beginning of the century, the youngest child often married *after* the death of at least one of his parents; today he marries some 15 or more years *before*. Children now are less and less born after their mothers are 30; and most women have finished childbearing by the age of 26 or 27. This, again, is a remarkable change by comparison with previous generations, when childbearing often continued at least until the mother was in her late thirties, if not right up to the menopause.

Infant and child mortality have declined. It is no longer necessary to conceive ten times to produce two teenagers. This has been accompanied by an increase in both knowledge about, and the efficiency of, contraceptive technology. The value set on family size has changed. This, like better contraception itself, seems to be related to the amount and quality of communication between the spouses. It is, in itself, an important indicator of the changed nature of marriage this century.

Those who protest against women being defined by their maternal role alone should note that the number of years a woman has to devote to this has declined dramatically – to perhaps about a seventh instead of a half of her life-span. If childbearing is over, for the statistically average woman, by 26, then her oldest child will be independent much sooner than when women were still bearing children in large numbers in their forties. With the increased life-expectancy of both spouses, this means that most marriages can expect at least two decades of child-free existence, as opposed to the five or six years 60 years ago. Peter Willmott has calculated that 'the "average" marriage, if wives outlived their husbands, lasted 28 years in 1911, and

42 years in 1967. If one assumes that children cease to be fully dependent at 15, then the period when the couple are largely alone has changed even more – from five years in 1911 to 23 years in 1967 ... in contrast with the earlier period, about as much of a couple's family life is now spent without dependent children as with.' Though these figures must be treated with caution, the trend they show is clear.

But what is the *meaning* of marriage? The marital state is, in general, more highly valued than any of the unmarried states, by both sexes of the appropriate age. Because of their social situation, this is even more true for women. Indeed, there does not seem to be an acceptable term that we all use by which we can speak of an unmarried woman, without conveying some feeling of disrespect and implied lower status. And unmarried men do not escape this totally. As the American sociologist, Ralph H. Turner, has pointed out: 'the attractive man or woman, with no discoverable personal deficiences, who fails to marry, represents a continuing puzzle to those about him, and is likely to be plagued with questions or insinuations about why he or she has not married.'

Since Durkheim, at least, sociologists have known that marriage is a key integrative mechanism in society. Indeed, Durkheim claimed to have shown that suicide varied inversely with the degree of integration of what he called domestic society. He demonstrated, for France in the 1890s, that the non-married had a suicide rate three times that of the married, that widowed persons killed themselves more often than married persons, but generally less than unmarried persons. Durkheim, though, had to point out that while marriage rates stayed the same in France during the nineteenth century, suicides had tripled, so he was forced to look elsewhere for evidence of the disintegration of society. Moralists have always been quick to equate divorce and marital break-up with the disorganization of society. Yet most divorcees re-marry; indeed, the spur to change one's legal status is usually the desire to re-marry. Typically, people divorce because marriage has become so important to them that they have no tolerance for the less than successful marriage they have contracted with the individual in question. There may well be *personal* disorganization, both as a cause and as a consequence of marital break-up. This, though, is quite a different matter and must be clearly distinguished by sociologists from *social* disorganization.

There are various rewards and penalties that sociologists associate with the married status itself.

First, and most simply, there is the prestige of being married. This is ritualized by one of the few remaining *rites de passage* in industrial society: the marriage ceremony. Credit ratings are higher if you are married. And if you are doing a bit of 'reality negotiation' with the police while you are being questioned late at night, to let drop that the lady with you is your wife is often enough to establish both credibility and respectability.

Related to the prestige, there are clear moral implications. In popular, and not so popular magazines, articles on bachelorhood and spinsterhood often have as a theme the duty to marry: people that don't are failing or shirking in some way. Often, too, the villains of the magazines' short stories are wilful, nay selfish, persons who refuse to marry. Another nauseating theme in women's magazines is marriage being gloried for its self-sacrifice. This is even to be found in some American texts on marriage and the family – for example, Willard Waller and Reuben Hill's *The Family*, which says: 'The pleasures of the married man are not heroic; but the curbing of self-indulgence, which married persons perpetrate upon themselves, has a kind of heroism about it.'

One of the most important rewards and/or penalties of marriage is what it means for your view of your own, and of other people's, personal competence – more than this, of their normality. There are few who could say that they have never suspected or labelled the unmarried as, in some way, disoriented or incompetent or maladjusted. Judgements about personal adequacy are being made when someone's marital status is asked about. Physical attractiveness is also being judged, especially for women: if you don't get married, haven't you been judged unattractive? For men, of course, unmarriage carries the association of homosexuality (an association which Kinsey, in his studies, supported).

The married state is statistically so 'normal' that, at the 1966 sample census, 87·2 per cent of all those aged between 30 and 49 were married. Marriage is seen as the normal accompaniment of maturity, when one supposedly stops the irresponsibility and immature behaviour of adolescence.

The act of demonstrating openly, to oneself and to others whose esteem one cares for, that one has achieved a given status is called, following G. H. Mead, *validation*. Marriage remains a key mechanism for 'validating' personal adequacy, heterosexual normality and personal maturity. People become anxious about all these three things when their marriage is unduly delayed – or when it fails and breaks up.

As this kind of mechanism, marriage varies in importance, of course, not only for different individuals but also between the sexes. It may well have generally declined in importance in the last decade, but most women are still denied alternative arenas for social validation – notably in careers – and so marriage remains more often needed by them than by men.

The question of validation explains why so many people (and, I suspect, more women than men) put up with not just the great inconvenience and unpleasantness, but also the unspeakable humiliation, of some marriages. They vest their identities in their marital status. So they submit to all this, rather than accept the clear demonstration that they have failed here.

What, then, *are* the consequences to the individual of the loss of a marriage? Research by Professor R. S. Weiss, of the Harvard Medical School, in both Boston and London, showed that widows – unlike widowers – did not want to consider another liaison for some time after bereavement. However, in the first year after bereavement, there is a greater amount of stress disease among men than among women; and widowers have more difficulty in maintaining their own routine than widows do.

These findings appear to be contradictory. They suggest, in the first place, that marriage is more important to women, but, in the second, to men. Weiss suggests that these and other anomalous findings can be resolved if marriage is considered to have several components, 'one of which evidences itself in *loyalty*, like that exhibited by faithful widows; another in *partnering*, which is what widowers seem so desperately to miss; another in *grief* on the loss of the marriage; and still another in *companionship* through the life of the marriage' (my italics). He further suggests that these components differ in their importance for men and women, in different class groups, and over a length of time as the marriage develops.

The factor of loyalty, or 'alliance', is common in anthropological literature. Rarely, in any society at any time, is marriage a relationship of purely personal concern to the persons thus joined together. It is often an alliance between groups of kin. There is a commitment among near kin to help one another, irrespective of the likelihood of being helped in return. Surviving spouses continue to feel responsibilities to the dead spouse : recently widowed women tend to repudiate new sexual ties, out of loyalty to their husband's memory. (Widowers re-marry sooner.) Widowed and divorced women express feelings of vulnerability and defencelessness. They feel, and indeed are, particularly vulnerable to community pressures.

Partnership, or collaboration, occurs mainly in managing the routine business of caring for the home and the children. For women, collaboration often seems important in maintaining their morale during endless and thankless housework. At the loss of a marriage, if they are at the appropriate age, women miss the relief from continuous child care that husbands meant. Dennis Marsden in his study, *Mothers Alone*, showed that mothers also found it hard to be the centre of both authority and affection for the children.

Women, however, seem able to do 'men's jobs' around the home. By contrast, men left with children seem less concerned about the responsibility or their morale, than about the mechanics of keeping the household going; they find housework difficult and burdensome. A widower with children tends to bring another woman into the home soon after his wife's death : housekeeper, mother or mother-in-law, or unmarried sister. And, in time, he will very likely have a second wife.

Grief at the ending of a marriage is, obviously, the corollary of the intimacy within it. Without marriage, the formerly married feel lonely, separate and emotionally empty. The divorced sometimes feel abandoned through their own unworthiness or through the wrongdoing of others. The bereaved often feel bitter at the unjust removal of the intimate one by a malign world. These feelings may be made worse by contact with others who seem to be more complete. The lack of a spouse, in Marsden's words, 'throws them out of key with married friends.'

Companionship in marriage is a relationship based on shared interests, which provide an exchange of information, evaluation and favours. It is based on years of co-presence and depends on a shared language. Peter Berger and Hans Kellner, in their article, 'Marriage and the construction of reality', argue that 'the reality of the world is sustained through conversation with significant others'; and, in this function, marriage has a special status for adults in our society. Marriage can be seen as a crucial 'nomic' (creating the opposite of the more familiar 'anomie') instrument in modern industrial society.

There are, naturally, differences in the levels of companionship in different social classes. Mirra Komarovsky has shown, in her *Blue-Collar Marriage*, that in working-class marriages in the United States companionship tends to drop off over time. The man becomes absorbed in work and sport, and the woman in the rituals of housework. This is, in fact, especially true after the birth of the first child, which produces a specialization of marital responsibilities.

At this time, it also becomes more difficult for the wife to maintain continuous companionship with other people outside the home – precisely because she has children. Therefore, as she becomes progressively more dependent on her marriage for companionship, she gets less.

One famous study of divorced women, William Goode's *After Divorce*, has shown that the divorced – especially women – have an equivocal position, at least in American society. Compared with a bereaved person, the divorcee lacks a clear role. The divorced do not have the 'standard package' of ties, obligations and identity, which are expected of adults and which make it easier for others to relate to them. This situation, Goode suggests, is one of the strongest pressures on the divorced to re-marry, so that they conform once again to the accepted patterns and thereby reinforce them.

Another reason for pressure towards re-marriage among the divorced is the sheer inconvenience of sexual pleasure outside marriage. As Goode wrote: 'Putting the matter in the most awkward way possible, given the boudoir facilities, working hours and social relationships within any given clique or circle, a couple must carry out detailed and clever plans if they wish to continue a sexual relationship without eventual marriage. The divorcee consequently finds any given sexual arrangements short of marriage increasingly inconvenient.' There have obviously been some changes since the early 1950s in Wayne County, Detroit, which was when and where Goode did his study. However, many ex-married people, while realizing that re-marriage is a solution to the problems of companionship and so on, fail to re-marry. The social activity of the widows – described for example by Peter Mariss and others – was so non-existent it was difficult to see how they could find a new husband. Similarly Marsden's study of husbandless, poor mothers, showed that marriage or re-marriage was contemplated as a solution by very few. Their social situation was usually such that they seldom met any marriageable men.

This emphasises that, in evaluating the significance to an individual of marital status, we must take note of related variables. Income matters: middle class divorced women lead very different lives from working class divorced ones. Age matters: the young and recently married lead different lives from the older and longer married. So does one's sex: the social situation of widowers differs markedly, as I have implied, from that of widows.

It is possible to see Weiss's four components of marriage

as causes for dissatisfaction. The kin obligations may be unwanted; partnership may be defined as nagging; the developments of the interlocking fantasy worlds of intimacy are unpredictable; companionship fades. But the strength of marriage – and the reason why 'married' is the most prestigious of the marital states – is that it remains the only relationship in which the positive gratification of all these components, in addition to the sexual and the paternal/maternal, are potentially available. I must not seem to play down sexual activity. Access to regular, legal, socially acceptable and comfortable sex is important in leading young people to get married in the first place, and in causing them to stay married. Nor should one underplay the drive to have children.

Paradoxically, however, marriage is a key integrative mechanism of society, largely because of its *privateness*. Because it is segregated from the 'public' institutions of work and the economy, of politics and real power, it is in the family and with marriage that people feel that they are master and have apparent power. Here, we are somebody not something. Berger and Kellner call the small family an 'innocuous "play area", in which the individual can safely exercise his world-building proctivities, without upsetting any of the important social, economic and political applecarts. Barred from expanding himself into the area occupied by these major institutions, he is given plenty of leeway to "discover himself" in his marriage and his family.'

This is a view of marriage as a very important social arrangement which creates for the individual the sort of order where he can experience his life as making sense. Deprive an individual of his significant Others and he will suffer *anomie* – i.e. he 'won't know where he is'. But their continued presence will sustain for him that *nomos* – that sense of identity – by which he can feel at home in the

world for most of the time. For most adults their most significant Other is their spouse.

Yet some people, we do not know precisely who, or how
many, in some family situations – again we do not know
precisely which – do not experience their family or marital
situation as making sense at all. As R. D. Laing, in particular, has taught us, the individual may indeed be reacting
'rationally' to the family situation despite being called
'mad' by near-relatives and psychiatrists. The *nomos* of
the spouses may be reaped as *anomie* by the children. This
noted, we should also realize that the limited work of
Laing has been widely extended by some far too readily to
all families – for example, to the extent that David Cooper
calls the family 'the gas-chamber of bourgeois society'.
It is in this form that the Laing/Cooper view is more of a
comforting ideology for the unhappily married, or recently
unmarried, radical intellectual, than proven sociological
fact.

Friends and Associates

'A man is known by the company he keeps.' Maybe so; but since 'birds of a feather flock together,' folk wisdom may not tell us very much. Studies of localities, or of stratification, demonstrate that like does indeed attract like; or, in Robert Merton's terms, there is 'status homophily' and 'value homophily' among friends. Sociology may appear to do little more than re-state the obvious. However, it does not take much thought for the topic to gain considerable complexity. Individuals in modern society do not occupy static and stable positions throughout their lives. They move physically and socially through many different spatial and social worlds. Those they work with need not necessarily be those they play with; marriage may, to some degree, unite families at different social levels; colleagues at one time may become subordinates at another; and so on.

We can think more clearly about this fluctuation in the range and intensity of an individual's associates through the notion of a 'social network'. Consider those people to whom we send Christmas cards, whom we invite to our parties or family ceremonies, or in any other way recognize as having some social significance in relation to ourselves. Let us call ourselves Person and individuals in the social network Others. Quite clearly, Person will not have seen all these Others equally often, with equal duration or with equal emotional intensity. Some may have been 'important' at previous periods of Person's life – for example, as employers, lovers or colleagues, and may have continued as 'friends' or acquaintances or simply names in an address book. The *meaning* of these Others to Person changes as Person gets older, wiser, richer, poorer or married.

Similarly, Others are themselves changing as they move biologically and socially through the various structures of life. Hence it is that, for many, to bring the recipients of their total Christmas card list into one room at one time would produce acute stress or anxiety. Others, who previously had remained in neat compartments or in specific roles – 'secretary', 'cousin', 'colleague', 'old school-friend', 'doctor', 'cleaning woman' or whatever is appropriate at a particular class-cultural level – come together and see something of Person's other identities.

We may *think* that we have some basic 'real me', which shines through, no matter with whom we are interacting. However, it is simply not possible 'to act the same with everyone', unless there is total and absolute congruence in life experience between all others concerned. But, of course, Person does not share Others' worlds: we may never discover, for example, what the word 'home' means to our spouse. Person has to modify what he (or she) says, or does, depending on the cues – language, gesture, expressions and so forth – which Other presents.

Thus, to return to the room full of the Christmas-card recipients of a given Person, it is evident that each Other will have received a different amount of Person's social investment, and will have slightly different ideas of 'who Person is'. Many are likely to think Person is acting 'out of character', or that he is, for example, 'buttering-up his mother-in-law', or 'pretending to be one of the boys', and so forth. That is Other clings to his *own* conception of Person, and to a degree disregards or devalues other identities which Person is displaying, and on which Other is, as it were, spying.

The more widespread use of the term, 'social network',

would help to underline the different levels and types of interaction between Person and Others. Many people interact with complete social equality only with their spouse or with very close friends.

This 'interactionist' approach to social behaviour sometimes receives moral disapproval from laymen, who may say that such an analysis implies that social behaviour is two-faced, calculating, 'being all things to all men', and so forth. Others might well argue, conversely, that such behaviour is sensitive, considerate, and sympathetic to others' needs and abilities. It is not helpful, when trying to be objective about the basic processes of social behaviour, to offer moral judgments about the nature of man. The point I am making is that social life is precarious and ambiguous, and that we do not behave as if all others are *exact* mirror-images of ourselves, nor as if they are so many cardboard role-players.

An individual's associates are largely a product of those factors that define an individual's life path – in particular, the type of job, or distinctive pattern of jobs, and the family life-cycle. Some people will stick with one job, one home, and one spouse, throughout life. Others will have a number (perhaps) of each, and will move between various places, and up and down various hierarchies. The tendency may be towards increasing disorderliness in these spheres. In the interstices between these structured spheres, an individual can create his 'own' world of friends and associates; but this very often involves extra effort. There are clear constraints imposed by certain Others on Person. Sex, religion, and skin colour, are obvious dividers. But in many work-groups – or indeed sport-groups – for a member to have his closest friends outside the group, is an implicit attack on the group's values.

The interaction of these 'structural' factors may be illustrated by the example of a middle-class housewife with

young children, moving into a new area as a result of a
move in her husband's job. She is isolated from previous
friends, family and familiar faces. Now she must pull in
new associates or 'friends' to fulfil certain functions –
someone to reinforce the value of her role as housewife
and mother; someone to reassure her that she has an identity separate from that of simply somebody else's wife;
and so on. Many such women are conditioned not to think
of themselves as having individual needs and expectations,
but rather to feel they must 'fit in' to whatever situation
they find themselves in. This may mean that a woman, not
knowing exactly what sort of person she ought to be, sets
out to make a relationship, the warmth and depth of which
she does not yet know, with another woman, about whom
she possesses little information and who is probably
equally unsure about what sort of person she herself is.

My discussion so far has assumed that Person's set of
Others is simply a series of dyads – groups of two – in
which Person is always a member. We now need to consider the so-called group effect. Since people do not generally find it rewarding to have the sustained disapproval of
a group with which they wish to be associated, there is
pressure to conform. This is particularly important for
understanding adolescent behaviour.

A number of studies have been concerned with how far
the adult values – as presented in schools – of success,
ambition, academic excellence and so forth, are under-
mined by membership in youth subcultures which centre
on out-of-school activities. Some of these studies have suffered from being too mechanistic. Involvement in youth
culture, like any other group activity, can be ritualistic
and segmental – i.e. performed without inner conviction,
so that Person may be in the group, but not wholly of it.
A mechanistic view of group influence on the individual
cannot be sustained.

An individual's behaviour is not necessarily influenced by the group of which he is a member. He may be more influenced by some other group or individual elsewhere. This idea is not a new one. Work by social psychologists and sociologists in the United States, during the 1940s and early 1950s, did much to clarify C. H. Cooley's statement, in *Human Nature and Social Order* (published in 1902), that the 'one who seems to be out of step with the procession is really keeping time to another music. As Thoreau said, he hears a different drummer ... The group to which we give allegiance, and to whose standards we try to conform, is determined by our own selective affinity, choosing among all the personal influences accessible to us.'

This brings up issues about the individual and the group. We are brought back to the process of mutual interaction. An individual's behaviour cannot be group-determined, if he chose his reference group from a range of alternatives; and, especially, if his choice is not a group of which he is a member. If the group is chosen by Person, then its 'constraints' may simply reflect individual 'choices'.

But even if the 'company he keeps' is an inadequate guide to Person's 'real' private plans and project, he must, as a social animal, orient his behaviour to some significant Other or group. The concept of 'reference groups' has stimulated research and analysis. Here is a recent definition of the term :

'In general, a reference group is a group, collectivity or person, which the actor takes into account in some manner, in the course of selecting a behaviour from among a set of alternatives, or in making a judgment about a problematic issue. A reference group helps to orient the actor in a certain course, whether of action or attitude.'

A *normative* reference group is the group from which a person takes his standards, or from which he derives his norms. Normative groups may include one's family, one's religion, one's nation, or individuals such as one's parent or one's spouse. An individual may conform with the norms put forward, or may deliberately act in exactly the opposite way from that which the normative group requires. What is important is that in some way or other, the norms of the reference group are affecting his behaviour.

A second type of reference group is the *comparative* group – the group whose situation or attributes a person compares with his own. If such a group is deprived in some way, by comparison with himself, an individual may feel a comforting sense of well-being. But if a comparative group is, in some important way, better off, this may give rise to feelings of 'relative deprivation'.

Perhaps the most famous study illustrating this point was S. A. Stouffer's work on *The American Soldier* published in 1949. Here it was shown that satisfaction was higher in the Military Police, where opportunities for promotion were not good, than in the Air Corps which had good promotion opportunities. Hence, in W. G. Runciman's words: 'The more people a man sees promoted when he is not promoted himself, the more people he may compare himself with in a situation where the comparison will make him feel relatively deprived.' Runciman's own exploration of reference groups and relative deprivation may be exemplified by his striking finding that 37 per cent of manual workers earning £10 or less in 1962, and 44 per cent of those earning between £10 and £15, could not think of others who were doing better in economic terms than they were. Quite evidently, reference groups were limited and localized. Analysis of this theme enabled Runciman to present a very persuasive case for the stability in British political life and the lack of wider radical movements based on a concern for social justice.

An important type of comparative reference group is the 'role model' from whom an individual learns how he (or she) should play his part. Thus, a married woman may adopt her mother as a role model; the student, his professor; the new factory worker, his bench mate.

Any one individual is likely to take into account reference groups of several different types; and perhaps he will be a reference group, or part of a reference group, for others. For a reference group to affect an individual's behaviour or attitudes, it is not necessary for it to exist in the present: a reference group, which has been very important for an individual in the past, or which he can see is going to be important to him in the future, may also be taken into account by him. Thus, a girl from a certain school may continue to behave as she feels the school expected, even though her personal links with the school have long since been severed, and the school itself now, in fact, expects different patterns of behaviour from its pupils. Similarly, a man who expects, and hopes, to attain to a higher level of management at work, may begin to behave in the ways which he considers such managers are expected to behave.

The environment in which men live is an order of things remembered and expected, as well as of things actually perceived. To understand what a man does, we must appreciate his definition of the situation. This requires knowing something of what he takes for granted. This is especially true in a 'pluralistic' society, where different people approach the same situation from diverse standpoints and where the same individual uses dissimilar perspectives in different transactions. Being able to identify the audience for whom a man is performing becomes a task of decisive importance.

Stress may arise when an individual is responding to conflicting reference groups, or when the members of a group, supposedly all in the same situation, are, in fact, responding to different reference groups. For example, dissent may arise in a parent/teacher association between the headmistress (among whose reference groups are the education authority and the association of head teachers), the teachers (whose reference groups include their fellow students at college and an image of 'teacher' as put forward by the mass media), and the parents (who have a multitude of reference groups, varying from their own parents, the members of other organizations of which they are also members, and so on). The members of the parent/teacher association may agree that it is 'the good of the children' which concerns them. But it would be impossible to understand their different views of what represents that 'good', and how it should be achieved, without some knowledge of the relevant reference groups.

The problems implicit in this approach appear in embarrassing profusion. Would it not be more appropriate to consider reference *individuals*, or role models, in many spheres, rather than reference *groups*? Such an individual may be Jesus, one's dead spouse or a much-admired teacher, known, perhaps, many years ago. Such internal models provide Thoreau's beat of a 'different drummer'. The knowledge that Jesus, or the deceased loved one, 'approves' attitudes and behaviour, which may be ridiculed by those immediately around the individual, provides the necessary social support.

It is crucial to clarify which aspects of behaviour follow from assumptions about 'people like us'. Any such category has clear assumptions about which spheres are legitimately open to the influence of others. Some questions, such as voting behaviour or other reasonably clear-cut issues, provide landmarks for those people seeking safe anchorage in a new identity.

It is, for example, widely known that most small

businessmen in Britain vote for the Conservatives, and they themselves know this. If they are Labour-voting, they generally know that they are 'deviant'. But, in many spheres, clear signals from reference groups or associates are often lacking. In those circumstances, an individual's behaviour may be inconsistent; his attitudes may be confused and ambiguous; and, on some issues, he is only likely to crystallize his views if persuaded to do so by a friendly sociologist on the doorstep.

The true distinction may be between those attitudes and aspects of behaviour that are defined in some way as 'private' or 'public'. The public ones lead to choices between conformity to, or deviation from, membership groups. In the 'private' sphere, there is no clear framework to deviate from. In this sphere, there may be a whole bundle of relevant reference groups and individuals. Though it may generally be possible to keep these various guides and reinforcers separate, there may often be considerable discordance or cross-pressuring. The final balance, struck by Person, is his own creative moulding of his 'true self'.

William James, in his *Principles of Psychology*, first published in 1890, put it admirably: 'I am often confronted by the necessity of standing by one of my empirical selves and relinquishing the rest. Not that I would not, if I could, be both handsome and fat and well-dressed and a great athlete, and make a million a year, be a wit, a *bon vivant*, and a ladykiller, as well as a philosopher, a philanthropist, a statesman, warrior, and African explorer, as well as "tone-poet" and saint. But the thing is simply impossible. ... So the seeker of his truest, strangest, deepest self must review the list carefully, and pick out the one on which to stake his salvation. All other selves become unreal, but the fortunes of this self are "real".'

One sociologist's warning that the concept of 'reference

group' is fast becoming a magic term, to explain anything and everything about group relations, appears to be warranted. Sociologists have usefully classified and categorized types of social relationships, and have indicated the processes of interaction between Person and Others. Now that it is part of our conventional wisdom to emphasize *relative* deprivation, and so forth, we may have done little more than reformulate the problem more precisely.

This need not be a cause for despair. Identification of the critical issue is the beginning of knowledge and understanding. Certain myths and half-truths are dispelled. We no longer have to believe in an over-socialized Person, moulded by his fellows, even as a highly malleable teenager. We know the strategies that are used to maintain autonomy; and we assume that such strategies are not necessarily limited by age and class, even though our minds do not all work like Marcel Proust's or Erving Goffman's.

One of the main difficulties, which remains unresolved, relates to the distinction which I made between 'public' and 'private'. And it may be that the existentialists are not completely wrong. We are what we choose to be. It is up to us to decide what influences will influence us – what we will regard as 'public' or 'private'. But what influences us to decide what we decide?

7 Michael Chisholm
Location

How much does an individual's mere address tell you about him? The world in general must think it important, because people so often try to maintain (say) that they live in Chelsea, whereas they really live in Fulham; or get worked up about the Post Office's giving them a postal address subsumed under the nearest town, instead of keeping their home-village differentiated; or, in conversation, try to distinguish between 'good' and 'bad' ends even of slum streets.

Address, too, is a crucial component of all census-taking and of most social surveys. But both sociologists and geographers are divided about the importance of location. The division usually is about precisely *what* it tells you. But there are those who dispute *whether* it tells you anything.

Let us take, as a central example, what has been written about cities, for we live in a predominantly urban society. Back in 1938, the American sociologist, Louis Wirth, published an essay on 'Urbanism as a way of life,' in which he argued that two important social processes operate in a city, but that one is triumphant over the other. Social segregation – the flocking together of like and like – was, in his view, a less powerful tendency than the process whereby diverse social groups, thrown into the urban melting pot, become progressively more alike.

Some twenty years later, H. J. Gans took issue with him, drawing the contrast between the inner city (which is what Wirth had studied) and the outer suburbs. Gans pointed out in, for example, *The Urban Villagers* and *The Levit-towners*, the undoubted demographic and social differences that exist within urban areas. Before Gans, between the two world wars, the Chicago school of sociologists had developed basic ideas about the social structuring of cities, and about the way that distinct zones or sectors emerge – slums or ghettoes; the zone of working men's housing; commuterland; and so on. Associated with each part of the city, it was postulated, is a distinct social class and style of life.

More recently, Melvin Webber has challenged the Chicago school's notion of the city, at least as the basis for planning the future. Webber expects greater personal mobility, and better communications, to allow any individual to have a wide range of social contacts, and to use the resources of the city, without there being geographical propinquity. (Webber, perhaps significantly, is at a Californian university, Berkeley. The planners of the midlands New City of Milton Keynes were much influenced by his ideas.) The whole concept of urban neighbourhood is, on Webber's argument, irrelevant – or is fast becoming so. Webber's homogenous city would, nevertheless, be inhabited by *individuals*, who would express their individuality by the particular style of life they chose.

Three views of the city: (a) everyone conforming to an urbanized stereotype; (b) individual, or at least group, identity expressed by social segregation; (c) an undifferentiated urban space in which everyone has the maximum chance to lead his own life. The truth seems to lie nearer (b) – the Chicago school/Gans image – than to either (a) or (c), both in the United States and in Britain. Because there is spatial differentiation within our cities, it is, in fact, useful to know of an individual where he (or she) lives. It will, at the very least, indicate the *probability* of his having various attributes.

Thus, the population of Greater London is very similar in its age-structure to the whole country. About 8 per cent are four years old or under; 13 per cent are five to fourteen years old, 40 per cent fifteen to forty-four; and the other 39 per cent are older. But, as the *Atlas of London*, published in 1971, shows dramatically, the proportions in the different age-groups vary widely from one part of London to another. In much of central London, around Charing Cross and west-wards thereof, less than 14 per cent of the local population is under fifteen. By contrast, east of the City – Bethnal Green,

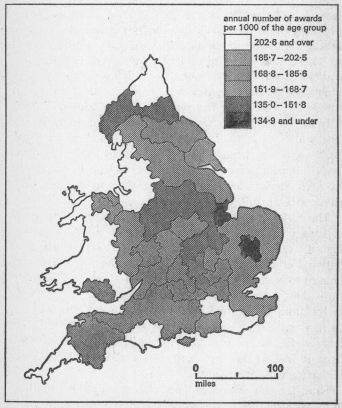

annual number of awards
per 1000 of the age group

202·6 and over
185·7 – 202·5
168·8 – 185·6
151·9 – 168·7
135·0 – 151·8
134·9 and under

0   100
miles

Figure 1   Awards for higher education : 1965-7

Stepney and beyond – runs a great belt of the conurbation where the population in this age-group rises to 45 per cent or more. Though the age-pattern in Greater London is generally a patchwork or mosaic, children are altogether more numerous in this eastern half, both north and south of the river Thames. In the much smaller city of Sunderland (population about 200,000), there are equally startling dif-

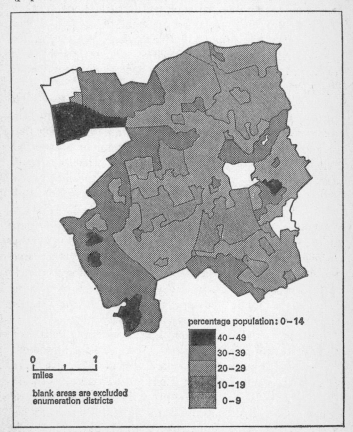

percentage population: 0–14

40 – 49
30 – 39
20 – 29
10 – 19
0 – 9

0   1
miles

blank areas are excluded
enumeration districts

Figure 2 Sunderland: distribution of persons aged 0-14

ferences in the population of young people (see maps.) In some census enumeration districts, almost half the population is (as in east London) fourteen or less, and the proportion falls to below 10 per cent elsewhere. In Sunderland, it is the western part that has the largest number of youngsters; central and eastern districts the least. Almost a mirror image of these patterns is the distribution of one-person households. In some parts of west-central London, they comprise anything up to 90 per cent of all households, compared with less than a tenth elsewhere. Where you live – where you can *afford*, as well as 'choose', to live – is associated with marital status, age and the number of your dependents.

As the Sunderland example helps to confirm, London is not exceptional in this kind of pattern, among either British or overseas cities. The differences are so striking that they are manifest in the bricks and mortar of towns. The high-density, fecund population of the Gorbals has traditionally lived in apartment blocks, while the more prosperous Glaswegian middle classes live in detached or semi-detached dwellings in Bearsden and Milngavie. Most of the students in lodgings in Bristol occupy bed-sitters or flats in the Redland and Clifton districts of imposing family residences that have now been subdivided. By the same token, there is usually little excuse for confusing a council housing estate with a private development. In a very literal manner, the urban landscape gives a clue to the kind of people who live in the various parts of a city.

Are you an owner-occupier, a local authority tenant, or the tenant of a private landlord? To return for a moment to London : owner-occupiers are almost non-existent in most of the centre between Charing Cross and Blackwall, but they account for a rising proportion of households as distance from this central area increases. They reach between 60 and 90 per cent in places like Bexley and Wembley. The distribution of immigrant communities is related to the pattern of tenure. Whether Irish or Jewish in the nineteenth century, or coloured in the twentieth, recent immigrants tend to cluster to the seedier quarters, often in privately rented accommodation; Notting Hill in London, or Balsall Heath in Birmingham, are present-day examples. Though, in due course, immigrants may join the drift to the suburbs, this is apt to take a generation or two. Within London, the Jewish dispersion from Whitechapel, through Stamford Hill, to Golders Green, is well documented. Now the Whitechapel streets that once housed Jewish immigrants house Pakistanis: will they move the same kind of way – and maintain the same group solidarity even while moving? We do not yet know.

Some kinds of social variation only come to light on very detailed inquiry. But this will show, for example, that there is even a geography of mental illness. A study published in 1971 showed that within London (inevitably a much studied city) there are striking differences in the number of inhabitants who have been discharged from hospital psychiatric care. In 1968, the rate per 10,000 of the resident population, in north east and east London, ranged from under 30, through the low forties for Haringey, to 61 in Stepney.

The spatial patterns are usually far from congruent. Thus, family size does not correlate well with rateable value or with form of tenure. Nevertheless, certain social characteristics are commonly found together. This is well illustrated by John Giggs's recent work on Barry (population around 40,000). With data for the 1959 census enumeration districts that covered the area of this south Welsh town, he examined the spatial patterns of phenomena that are symptomatic of social disorder: the proportion of the population suffering from tuberculosis; the number of credit delinquents; people convicted of offences against property; and so on. He found that social malaise, as measured by these thirteen variables, was concentrated in the

inner and eastern parts of Barry. In the Barry Dock and
Cadoxton areas, however, there was a large continuous region of little social disorder, which, interestingly, straddled
inner, intermediate and suburban areas. The most thorough
study of any British town using Gigg's multivariate techniques is Robson's 1969 analysis of Sunderland, from which my
earlier example was drawn. From the Sunderland data, he
extracted various important components, including class,
age and quality of housing. When mapped, the components showed considerable spatial regularity, especially
quality of housing; this shows a concentric zoning, with
poor housing, a feature of the central city, as is true elsewhere.

Cities, of course, do not only differ internally, they also
differ from one another in all kinds of ways. Bristol, for
example, has something like 107 'households' for every
100 dwellings, whereas Bootle is in equilibrium, at a ratio
of one to one. The classic study of these variations in Britain is Claus Moser's and Wolf Scott's *British Towns: a
statistical study of their social and economic differences*.
They took all the towns that had a population of more
than 50,000 in 1951 and undertook multivariate analysis
on a very large number of variables. They identified six
important components, to which a recognizable meaning
could be attached in four cases. The two most important
were the components that measured social class and urban
growth in the years 1931–51. These yielding some very
interesting groupings of cities. Towns of high social class
like Bath, Cambridge, Oxford, Exeter and Maidstone had
had little growth. At the other extreme, both low social
class and a rapid expansion characterized Scunthorpe,
Rotherham and Wigan. Moser's and Scott's analysis showed how towns that recognizably share economic characteristics also share social attributes. The Yorkshire wool
textile towns of Halifax, Dewsbury and Leeds, and the

Lancashire cotton towns of Oldham, Burnley and Bolton, come together here. They have similar educational and housing characteristics.

A special class of town, not considered by Moser and Scott, is the group designated as New Towns. It is widely believed that, despite their initial intentions, these have become socially unbalanced, almost one-class towns, inhabited only by better-paid manual workers. This belief is reinforced by the concern expressed by the development corporations on this score. In the case of Milton Keynes, it is written into the plan that strenuous attempts should be made to ensure social balance in the community. How this will work out in practice remains to be seen, as only forty-two houses had been completed by June 1971.

At first sight, the census data do not confirm any very startling differences between the social structures of the New Towns and the rest of the country. In 1966, the London New Towns had 16·1 per cent of their economically active population in the categories 'employers', 'managers' and 'professional workers', compared with 14·6 per cent for England and Wales as a whole. Likewise, skilled and semi-skilled workers constituted 49·8 per cent and 46·2 per cent respectively. But the census data hide important social facts within their broad categories.

In the first place, practically all the New Towns are dominated by factory employment, so much so that the development corporations are seeking to diversify into office jobs. Thus, the *kinds* of managerial and professional worker probably differ socially from their counterparts in many other places. Second, the industries that have set themselves up in the New Towns are the expanding engineering, electronic and related industries, which in general pay good wages. There are no comprehensive statistics on incomes for individual New Towns, but car ownership is a good indicator. Around London, the New Towns have 61 per cent of households owning at least one car, compared with 46 per cent for England and Wales. Away from London, the New Town car-ownership level is much nearer the national average, but is mostly well above the rate for the locality in which the New Town is situated. This indicates a high level of prosperity relative to the region. Third, the great majority of immigrants to the New Towns are young couples, so that the age-structure is heavily biased downwards. So it is likely, whatever the census says, that if you live in a New Town, you are reasonably well-off, have a young family, and do some sort of job in a factory. And, if this is not true of you individually, this is the environment to which you (and your children) must relate.

Regional differences in economic and social conditions are very marked. Coates and Rawstron have brought together a mass of data on personal incomes, educational opportunities, health and other matters, to demonstrate this. The map shows the variation in higher education opportunities. The data in the table show the nature and magnitude of these various geographical differences, and the dramatic effect they have on weekly family expenditure. 1967–8 represent the last years of relatively 'normal' conditions before the inexorable rise of unemployment to the million mark in January 1972, a national average in excess of 4 per cent.

Lying behind these regional differences is the spatial variation in kinds of employment. At the extreme, Corby and Port Talbot are not only one-industry but one-firm towns, dependent on a single steel plant. The upper Clyde is dominated by shipbuilding, and even Bristol has an uncomfortably large number of eggs in one basket – 40,000 workers in the manufacture of aircraft. The classes of skill required differs from industry to industry (so does the proportion of women to men workers). Thus, if there is a long shadow over both ships and aircraft, workers in the aircraft industry will have less need of government re-training than shipyard workers.

Nor are these regional differences changing much. Analysis by M. Chisholm and J. Oeppen of the University of Bristol of employment data for the 61 economic planning subregions of Great Britain shows that, between 1959 and 1968, there was surprisingly little change in the pattern of jobs available locally, despite massive government investment in regional policies. And the level of unemployment has remained obstinately high in particular areas, notably Northern Ireland and Scotland, for most years since the second world war.

It is now a recognized fact that opportunities in life are affected by where an individual is born. The Educational Priority Areas policy is one manifestation of this, with its attempt to improve the worst schools in urban areas – often in the central parts of cities, but sometimes in a mining village like Denaby in the West Riding of Yorkshire. To some extent, migration reinforces these initial differences; the better educated tend to move away from areas of poor opportunities. The migration process is slow, and it operates through short moves more commonly than long-distance ones. However, a process of spatial sorting does go on, tending to reinforce, rather than obliterate, the geographical differences that have been noted.

The 1966 sample census showed that almost 10 per cent of the United Kingdom population had moved house within the twelve months before the census, and 31 per cent within the previous five years. (Mobility is increasing, but is nowhere near American levels yet.) About half the moves were within the local authority – i.e. fairly short-distance; about half were moves between authorities – i.e. a mixture of short- and long-distance. Though the gross flow is large, the net balance for any area is a small fraction of this. Scotland, with the most serious problem of net emigration of any of the standard regions, had a net loss by migration of 16,000 in 1966. This was made up of a gross outflow of 53,000 and an inflow of 37,000.

Table 1 *Regional Variations: Jobs, Income, Expenditure*

Standard region	average unemployed 1968 %	activity rates (males + females) 1968 %	annual income per taxpayer 1967–8 £	weekly family expenditure per person 1967–8 £
Northern Ireland	7·2	48·9	976	6·60
north	4·7	51·8	1086	7·65
Wales	4·0	47·1	1103	7·50
Scotland	3·8	56·4	1094	7·55
Yorkshire and Humberside	2·6	56·1	1113	7·25
north west	2·5	58·1	1103	7·95
south west	2·5	47·0	1130	7·95
west midlands	2·2	60·2	1180	8·05
East Anglia	2·0	48·5	1115	8·10
east midlands	1·9	56·3	1152	7·55
south east	1·6	59·7	1258	9·25

Source: Central Statistical Office, *Abstract of Regional Statistics*, No. 6, 1970

The geographical patterns of movement are fairly complex, but two important elements can be discerned. The first is the flight from the central areas of the major cities. All the conurbations are losing population (this is partly a function of people's higher demands for spacious housing); and the Greater London Council is now worried whether the trend will be checked without the government changing its policy of channelling jobs to other regions. There is a much greater chance of being an in-migrant in the suburbs than in the city centre. Immigrants into Bristol (as defined by the formal city boundary) within the year before the 1966 census accounted for only 3·4 per cent of all the city's inhabitants; but in neighbouring Thornbury (formerly a rural district authority; in fact, an exurb), the proportion was four times as great, at 12·5 per cent. Here, it was not a case of overspill from the city but net growth on the periphery.

The second feature of migration – inter-regional transfers – now has a less distinct pattern than in the earlier postwar years, when the drift to the south east of Britain seemed well-established and irreversible. In fact, the south east is now losing population by migration, and it is the south west that is the major gainer. Though Scotland remains a region of substantial loss, for most other regions inflows balance outflows. Nevertheless, some striking regional contrasts exist. Within the counties of Glamorganshire and Monmouth – the main industrial area of south Wales – only Cwmbran, with 11 per cent of in-migrants within the last few years, even approaches Thornbury's 12·5 per cent, and Cwmbran is a New Town. No other local authority in these two counties exceeded 8·9 per cent of in-migrants. For towns like Rhondda, subject to steady migration loss, the proportion who had migrated in during the past few years was barely 1 per cent.

Something like four fifths of the British population lives in urban areas, hence my concentration on urban patterns. Indeed, most people living in the country are no longer country-dwellers in the traditional manner; comparatively few work on the land or in associated industries. Many rural dwellers commute daily to the cities, or are weekenders retreating therefrom to their second home. Except for crofting communities in Scotland, and farmers in such remote areas as the Pennines and central Wales, one cannot in Britain really distinguish a rural from an urban habit of life. The fact is that to live in the real countryside is increasingly the prerogative of the relatively wealthy. With the decline and imminent demise of rural public transport, it is at least essential to run a car. Work is locally available only for a few, and the journey to work in nearby towns and cities is not cheap. On the other hand, a hundred years ago the countryside provided a major pool of low-paid workers (the function that it still fulfils in later-industrialized countries like France or Italy); this is no longer so in Britain. The major concentrations of the very poor are in the city centres, though some notable rural slums exist, on (for example) some caravan sites.

Wirth's analysis may be true of city centres, then. Webber's predictions seem to lie in a far future. All the evidence shows that there are distinct social groupings both within and between cities and that these may be changing but they are not vanishing. Even if the spatial patterns do not take on a regularity that theorists would like (they are both complex and overlapping), knowing where a person lives tells one a good deal not only about the kind of person he or she is likely to be now, but also something about their children's life-course. The work that is beginning to be done on people's mental images of their own neighbourhood and other places, shows that they themselves perceive localities in quite explicit terms and relate them to what they think is an appropriate setting for themselves as individuals or as members of a family. And whether the image resembles 'reality' is not so important as the fact that most people identify themselves with one (spatially segregated) social group, and thereby differentiate themselves from other (also spatially segregated) groups. Unfortunately, though, it is much harder to probe what is in the mind than to measure what is on the ground.

8 Philip Abrams
Age and Generation

There are societies in which to know a man's age is to know almost everything about him. By contrast, the extent to which age controls an individual's social role and status (or even indicates them) in advanced industrial societies is extraordinarily slight. And this despite all the writing about 'youth culture' and the 'generation gap'.

Yet, in survey research, information is sought about age more frequently and systematically than about any other variable. A survey of surveys carried out in Britain, Europe and the United States in 1965 found that age was, at that time, the background variable on which information was most regularly collected in survey research. The institutions sampled included government departments, academic research institutes and market research organizations. In Britain alone, there were then eighty-two agencies conducting survey research regularly; they completed between them about two million interviews a year; and at least one question on age was included in every case.

The age-profiles of whole populations (i.e. what proportions fall into certain age-brackets) can, of course, be got at with great ease through survey research, and they provide first-class information for describing society (explanation is a different matter). Because age, as a matter of common sense, indicates the point a person has reached in the process of *biological* maturation and development, population age-profiles are an easy way of mapping certain kinds of *social* problems. Within limits, age-profiles are also a means to project future maps of those problems. Census authorities and insurance companies have always made successful use of age data in this way. Population projections have, of course, had a nasty habit of going wrong in the event – because, for example, no allowance was made for the effect of economic change on people's attitudes to the 'value' of children. Nevertheless, of the three elements on which such population projections are normally based – namely, estimates of migration, estimates of mortality, and estimates of births – estimates of births have proved the most important and the most reliable; and they are derived directly from data about the current age-distribution of the population.

The essential item of information is the number of women of child-bearing age. Largely because we know already that this total is certain to increase in the next 30 years, we can assert, with all the demographer's traditional confidence, that an increase in the population of the United Kingdom towards a figure of 66 million by the end of the century, is virtually inescapable. It follows from the numbers of young people already in the population, the potential parents of the 1970s and the 1980s.

A similar use of gross age-profile statistics allows one to identify and to project the 'dependency-ratios'. What is being mapped, in this type of exercise, is the size of the groups in a population which, on account of their age, will have to be supported by others. We can obtain not just the scale of the dependency-ratio but also its constitution – how much of it is made up of the very young, and how much of the very old, or of those who are effectively dependent because they are fully engaged in unpaid work caring for the very young or the very old.

One of the first people to realize the social relevance of simple age-profile data was Seebohm Rowntree. In the face of the vigorous advocacy (by Charles Booth and the Webbs) of universal old age pensions as a panacea for poverty, Rowntree showed, in the final chapter of his *Poverty: a study of town life*, that the contribution of old age pensions to eliminating poverty would, at that time, have been depressingly slight. The age-distribution of the population of the poor revealed, only too brutally, that the core, as well as the bulk, of the poverty problem in 1890 was at the other end of the dependency-ratio. It was a problem of child poverty: 44 per cent of the poor were below the age of fifteen. By contrast, the age-distribution of the population projected for the end of this century, though having the same pyramid shape as that found at the end of the last century, is going to be strikingly fatter at the top – i.e. a very much larger proportion of the dependent population will be old.

Rowntree's work is an early, clear example of the way in which age data gain a social, as distinct from a biologi-cal, meaning. Perhaps the most cogent passage of *Poverty* is that section of chapter five where the author demon-strates how the *social* organization of the life-cycle (chil-dren do not earn) compounds the problem of poverty which is induced through directly *biological* dependence (children have to be reared). His discovery was a dramatic step beyond the use of age-data till then common in de-mographic research. It also had dramatic implications for policy. Anyone looking at Rowntree's chart (see Figure 1), in which he expresses the life-cycle as a series of age-specific waves of poverty and affluence, can see that the periodic reductions of well-being are consequent not only on biology, but also on the market and on the kinship sys-

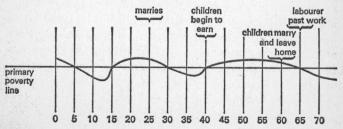

Figure 1

tem. The life-cycle is, in important respects, a social arte-
fact. Universal public nurseries, communal living, reform
of the family – these could change the social meaning of
age. But, of course, they have not done so yet. The individual life-cycle lies somewhere between that which
Rowntree studied and the projected end-of-century pattern. At the moment, we still need a Child Poverty Action
Group. But Brian Abel-Smith recently pointed out that
services for the old will increasingly demand 'the major
part of social security expenditure'.

The type of understanding of the social meaning of age
achieved by Rowntree has been effectively put to use in
market research as well as in social policy. The relationship of age to income, and to consumer behaviour, is one
of the most reliable bases for creating and exploiting new
markets. What is observed is simply what Rowntree observed – stood on its head. There are age-specific periods in
the life-cycle, when people whose income is normally
tightly committed find they have money to spend. The
most exploitable of these periods – because it is not overshadowed by the memory of earlier periods when income
was committed – is early adulthood, between starting work
and having children. Or, in the terms in which the data
normally come up from the machine-room in survey research, from ages fifteen to twenty-nine.

We shall probably never be able to show just how far
the explosion of youth culture in Britain in the 1950s was
a direct consequence of commercial opportunism, responding to this discovery. But many organizations involved in
marketing clothes and music have admitted frankly how
important the discovery of the teenage-plus consumer has
been in revolutionizing their production strategies in the
past twenty years.

What the research had revealed was an enigmatic correlation. People in this age-category not only had dispos-

able income above their immediately felt needs, but also could be induced to respond in a uniquely sensitive way to the appeals of fashion. For this age-category, the idea of newness could be given very positive resonance. The *explanation* of this relationship is not something which research of this type is likely to bring to light. It involves a deeper look at the social organization of age than one needs in order to make successful decisions about the marketing of a new magazine or a new singer. Predictability, not understanding, is all that this type of research requires or produces.

The 1971 campaign against cigarette smoking was centred on the idea that smoking is out of date, peculiarly associated with being middle-aged. It was a shrewdly calculated campaign. But I doubt whether its sponsors could point to any survey research that explains *why* it was likely to work. They might, however, point to Georg Simmel's wholly speculative essay on fashion, first published in 1904. The force of the idea of fashion. Simmel argued, lies in the way it combines innovation with imitation. It permits individuals to distinguish themselves from others, not as isolated or eccentric individuals, but as members of a fashion-leading group. In a society where people are already predisposed to identify themselves in terms of age, the association of the idea of fashion with that of youth could become a powerful source of real social change.

Political sociology gets a bit closer to explaining the social meaning of age than either demographic or market research has normally done. This is not so much as a result of the theoretical interests of political sociologists as because, for commercial polling agencies, age is a standard variable. A very high proportion of research in political sociology is carried out for academics by commercial polling agencies. So researchers found themselves confronted with large numbers of tabulations relating age to voting behaviour. The problem was to discover what the tables meant.

To begin with, the tables were allowed to speak for themselves; and what they said was, for the most part, pretty trivial. In *How People Vote* (1956), Benney, Pear and Gray found that age made little difference to interest in politics, though there did appear to be some truth in the old adage about being radical in youth and conservative in old age. Using a single age-break – 21–49 on the one side, 50 and over on the other – they found that in Britain the old of all social classes were measurably more likely to vote Conservative than the young.

The old adage still has wide currency in political research, as has the commonest explanation of it – that it is the biological and psychological process of aging that itself produces the growing conservatism. Thus, in *The American Voter* (1962), one of the best of the more recent voting studies, Campbell, Converse, Miller and Stokes say: 'There is, furthermore, a substantial tendency for conservatism to increase with age, as we might expect on commonsense grounds.' Elsewhere, however, these same authors are properly sceptical about commonsense expectations. Studied more carefully, the tables complicate the issue (there is, for example, the problem of the differential mortality rates of different social classes; the old are disproportionately middle class) and they begin to produce puzzles and contradictions which cannot be accepted at face value. There is the finding that the young are more likely to change party allegiance in any given election campaign than the old, and the finding that the older you are in electoral experience the more likely you are to have changed allegiance. To make sense of the data, the idea of the 'political generation' was invoked. Crucial here is not how old you are, but *when you were young*.

The classical version of this strategy was adopted by

Berelson, Lazarsfeld and McPhee in their *Voting* (1954).
They say: 'The younger generation raised in the New Deal
era showed a high tendency to vote along the socio-
economic class lines associated with the Roosevelt elections.' They develop this into an elaborate theory: 'A
whole political generation may have been developing, for
whom the socio-economic problems of their youth served
as bases for permanent political norms – a semi-permanent
generation that would later bulge the ranks of the Demo-
crats in certain age groups, much as the crop of postwar
babies is bulging different grades in school as they grow
up. Presumably an age-generation can be transformed by
political events and social conditions into a political
generation ... a generation that retains its allegiances and
norms while succeeding generations are moving in another
direction.'

This strikes me as a good explanation. But it is entirely
unsupported by the survey research. The same line of explanation has, nevertheless, been developed in more recent
studies – most conspicuously by Butler and Stokes in their
Political Change in Britain (1969). This study reveals, I
think, more clearly than any other single work just how
far survey research can take us in understanding the social
meaning and organization of age; and where it almost
necessarily breaks down.

The importance of the Butler and Stokes book (not only
for political sociology) is that the authors appreciate that
the problem of generations lies in linking personal time
(the life-cycle) with social time (history). They suggest four
ages in the life of political man. First, there is a time of
infant innocence, devoid of meaningful political information, but in which a good deal of very salient emotional
colouring for later political learning is absorbed from one's
immediate family environment. Then, there is the period
of childhood, adolescence and young adulthood, in which

politics is first directly perceived, and in which relationships to politics are worked out in a way which is partly calculating, partly shaped by the persuasive subterranean influence of close emotional attachments to family and friends. After this phase of relative plasticity and political experiment, there comes the phase of adult life proper, in which commitments harden and settle, and interest in politics tends to increase. Finally, in the phase of old age, political allegiances are typically strong though interest in politics, other than in issues specifically related to the situation of the elderly, declines.

All of this is well supported by a large body of research over and above that of Butler and Stokes themselves. It is the next step that is critical, and far less secure. They seize on the fact that the second phase of the political life-cycle is the one in which people are most susceptible to change, most capable of responding in new ways to events; most in the market, as it were, for a political identity. They then suggest that British history since 1880 reveals four great, and very distinct, phases of political action and crisis. People who were in the second phase of their political life-cycle during each of these distinct phases of political history have, it is argued, developed distinctive patterns of orientation to politics, which have in important ways stayed with them ever since. A sophisticated statistical demonstration of the plausibility of this argument follows. What does not follow is any serious effort to find evidence to support the Butler and Stokes assumptions, true though they may be. To pin down the social meaning of age, we need both a different sort of evidence and, more important, a different sort of theory from that which is normally found in political sociology. One place where these do sometimes turn up is in the mass of recent sociological and psychological writing on 'the problem of youth', or, more specifically, on 'youth and unrest'. Here the issue of generations is addressed much more directly.

What survey research offers us here is, in the first place, a number of seeming paradoxes. In industrial and industrializing societies, age-stratification – i.e. the distributions of power derived from, and legitimated by, differences of age – diminshes. At the same time, generational conflict – i.e. the appeal to age as a proper basis of social differentiation, and of demands for equality – increases. Youth becomes an ideological symbol and a categorizing label of great force, for both old and young, in just those societies where the fact of being young is least likely to be treated as a sufficient determinant of a person's status or destiny. In societies where the movement from being a child to being an adult takes a single day, and is marked by highly ritualized ceremonies of passage and recognition, this phase of the life-cycle cannot become problematic, in the way it is when the same passage is an unstructured, open-ended experiment lasting for an indefinite number of years. The studies of protest tell us *both* that age data will not serve to identify the protest-prone, *and* that those actively involved in protest movements are concentrated in particular age categories.

In practice, the way in which scholars such as Karl Mannheim, S. N. Eisenstadt and, in a rather more modest context, Frank Musgrove, have conceived of the problem of generations cuts through these difficulties quite easily. What we are faced with is a situation of relative deprivation. Age-stratification is diminished but not eliminated. And because age is discredited as a legitimate or effective basis of equality, those de-facto age-linked inequalities that remain are seen as a legitimate focus of discontent. Yet discontent is voiced not by whole age-categories, but by particular groups or groupings within an age-category who are experiencing some predicament of the category as a whole in a particularly acute way. Mannheim calls these groups 'generation units'.

It is always youth-related-to-something-else that locates the sources of protest, not just youth in itself: age plus family background, plus educational experience, plus race, plus class, for example. We do not find many social phenomena which are universal to any given age-category. But we find many phenomena for which membership of a particular age-category – say, youth – is a necessary condition for their occurrence. In the case of youth, most of these are phenomena of change: cultural innovation, migration, revolution, fashion.

It is at this point that something like the social psychology of the life-cycle developed by Eric Erikson (theory), combined with close case-study and observational research (evidence), rather than yet more conventional surveys, seem to me to be called for. Take, again, the 'political generation' question: when was it the voter was young? Being young is, in many ways, a matter of identification (some people, notoriously, were 'never young'); but it also involves the respondent's sense of place in history. I have seen no survey which puts that problem into an answerable question.

Another set of studies is worth mentioning here. Gerontology, the study of old age, is one of the relatively advanced specialized social sciences. The problem faced by gerontologists is basically a biological one, of course – the return to dependency with the decline of faculties and powers in age. But the problems of isolation, of the withdrawal of interest from the outside world, of the difficulties older people have in adjusting to the accelerating pace of life in society as a whole – these are socially induced to a high degree. That is to say, it seems that our sort of society systematically aggravates certain biologically based pre-dispositions associated with aging to the point of turning them into quite acute social problems.

Here again what we are often faced with is not just a problem of biological age, but a problem of the relationship of personal time to historical time. Thus Alvin Toffler has suggested, in his *Future Shock*, that we may never solve these problems until we find the means 'through' biochemistry or re-education either to alter old people's time sense, or to provide structured enclaves for them in which the pace of life is controlled, and even, perhaps, regulated according to a 'sliding scale' calendar that reflects their own subjective perception of time.'

Studies of the relationship between age and leisure and of the problems of mid-career technical obsolescence tend to confirm this view. Once again what we observe are not effects which are absolutely linked to age, not necessary concomitants of points in the life cycle, but problems induced by our particular culture in particular phases of the life cycle. The lesson, again, is that what we should be studying is not this or that bit of the life-cycle in isolation, or correlated to this or that particular activity, but the social context and organization of the life-cycle as a whole. All those statistics – on variations in (say) TV watching or talking to friends with age – only describe our problem. How are we to get into the dynamics of ageing as a bio-cultural process?

Fortunately the picture is not totally blank. One means of getting more information data is the longitudinal, as opposed to the simple cross-sectional, survey. Seymour Martin Lipset and Everett Carll Ladd Jr have showed how effective even approximation to this technique can be. Lipset and Ladd used a succession of single cross-sectional surveys to create a quasi-longitudinal study, in order to investigate the relationship between age and political attitudes over a 40-year period. They found that there has been

a 'historical slope' towards the left in the attitudes of suc-
cessive generations of college-educated Americans, but that
this has been offset by what could be called a 'biographical
slope' towards the right within the life-cycle of each particular generation. The *net* move to the left over the whole
period, and for the foreseeable future, is thus much less
than cross-sectional studies of the young on their own
would suggest.

When we turn to longitudinal studies proper – to that
body of research which, having selected a population on
the basis of chronological age, then studies that population
at frequent and regular intervals over long periods of time
– we find a rich body of information. Some of the best of
this work has been done in Britain, for example by the
Medical Research Council team headed by J. W. B. Douglas, and in the National Child Development Study directed
by Professor N. R. Butler. Though studies of this type use
chronological age as an initial basis of sampling, their
focus is not on age as such but on tracing sequences of
development, and on establishing correlations between
these sequences and a wide range of variables which are
also treated longitudinally.

The pay-off in terms of firm data has already been enormous. Research of this kind gives us a means of isolating
the significance of age, as distinct from, say, the phasing
of experience in an individual's life. This is a very important distinction. The longitudinal studies cast doubt on
the notion, derived from earlier clinical psychology, of
critical ages in personality development. They substitute
for it the much more permissive idea of an *optimal phasing*
of processes of development.

This raises again the problem of self-definition. Many
studies have shown that individuals may identify themselves as being 'of' a particular generation in ways which
can be startlingly unrelated to their actual biological age.

The most interesting versions of this are the people who manage to be 'young after their time' (the 40 year old hippy). More familiar is the man who is 'old before his time' — who seems to have been over-socialized into the roles and responsibilities of middle age, when most of his contemporaries are still sowing wild oats. The 'too old' self-definition seems to be especially common in people born to older parents. The 'too young' self-definition seems associated with an unfulfilled quest for satisfactory intimate personal relationships of the kind usually formed in late adolescence.

But the real research on this remains to be done. My own guess is that closer studies of the phasing of critical experiences will give us the answers we want.

9 Alan Little
Education

This book starts with a number of questions that Frank Bechhofer, discussing income, found commonplace in Britain. Questions like 'What does he do?' 'How does he earn his money?' In my experience these questions are often heard, but less frequently than variants of 'Where did he go to school?' or, even more often, 'Where are your children going to school?' I have never, in any other country, come across the frequent and intensive questioning about the places where people were, or children are, being educated.

In other countries, the quality of an individual's education may well be discussed, but not where it is taking place. For the British, at least, where you went to school appears to be as important as what you did there, or how well you did it. This is perhaps the contemporary Englishman's vice. But what does education do for us? How does the type of education, its level and quality and where you went, affect you? In terms of specific technical questions: how far is it the determinant of the sort of people or the type of society we are? Or, does education merely reflect and reinforce other more basic features of ourselves and of our society?

An appropriate starting point is the way education places us in society and, in particular, enables us to earn a living. The evidence on this is clear-cut: a consistent and striking correlation between length of schooling and earnings. In the United States, thanks to the inclusion of both income and educational questions on the census, the documentation of this relationship is voluminous. Twenty years ago, middle-aged American men (aged 35 to 54), who had completed college, earned 80 per cent more per year than their counterparts who had graduated from high school; and 160 per cent more than those people whose education had finished after elementary schooling. Unfortunately, British evidence is more limited in both detail and frequency. Nevertheless, a follow-up study of respondents to the 1966 sample census has been completed by the Department of Education and Science and gives some information about earnings: whereas in 1966 the average earnings of 40 year old men was around £1250, people with Higher National Certificate earned roughly £1800, and those with degrees earned over £3000.

The problem is, however, not so much with facts like these as with their interpretation. The more educated certainly seem to earn more than the less educated. But is this primarily because education enhances one's job performance (in other words, gives us skills that are useful to employers), or is education's role symbolic and ritualistic rather than real? One point that is frequently ignored when people consider the relationship between education and income is that, until quite recently, education (and, in particular, prolonged education) was a rare experience. It is only in the last decade or so, and in a few countries, that prolonged secondary or higher education has become the experience of a substantial minority of the population. Traditionally, both were the experience of privileged groups. If employers were either snobbish, or assumed that the more schooling a person had, the better the worker he was likely to become, this might explain at least some of the relationships between earnings and education. Further, it might lead us to foresee that, as education becomes more of a mass experience, its relationship with earnings will decline. However, it must be admitted that, in the United States, there is no evidence to suggest that the empirical relationship between length of schooling and earnings is weakening. What does seem to be happening is that the differences are between later steps in the educational staircase than in the past. On top of this, many critics have made a distinction between education (i.e. length of schooling) and learning (the collection of experiences which contribute to a person's knowledge and skill). The former is a school experience, while the latter stems from a variety of sources in society, of which full-time education is only one.

It is interesting to note that the problem of interpreting an empirical relationship between individual earnings and education, is paralleled, on the national level, by the relationship between global expenditure on education and levels of economic development and growth. There is no disputing the facts; the richer the country, the greater its human resource development and the larger its expenditure on education. F. Harbison and C. A. Myers's study, *Education, Manpower and Economic Growth*, is one of many that have highlighted the empirical relationship. But how should we interpret it? Are countries richer because they spend more on education – which is the way advocates of education would argue. Or do rich countries spend more because they are richer and the population demands it? In principle, it is the same chicken-and-egg problem as whether or not what a child brings to school is more significant than what he receives there. Unfortunately, it is not only an 'academic' problem, but has profound complications for anyone depending on strategies for resource allocations in developing countries.

The idea that the contribution schooling makes to earning potential is to reinforce other aspects of the individual, is important. The most obvious of these aspects are certain facets (either intellectual or personal) that are of considerable economic or social usefulness and are also talents associated with school performance. To put it simply, clever people and/or hard workers do well at school *and* at work.

On this view, education may focus the cleverness, or any other capacity, by giving it something to 'work on', but it neither radically changes, creates nor significantly adds to it. Further, it is these capacities that employers want (or ought to want) rather than education. There is a lot of strength in this argument, scarcely weakened by employers' increasing demand for 'certificates' of one kind or another: as prolonged education becomes more general and exams come under attack, these are increasingly likely to become simple attendance certificates, not level-of-competence credentials.

Again, there is no need here to document the narrow socio-economic background that the traditionally educated come from. Yet this kind of correlation is crucial for the sort of person the individual is, and becomes. It is at least arguable that the type of skills that employers have wanted, and have been prepared to pay for, were as much the result of these backgrounds as of the education individuals had benefited (or suffered) from. What these arguments have in common is that they suggest more fundamental questions about a person than his education. You may be able to tell a Balliol man anywhere; but this is not so much the influence of Balliol as of what was necessary to get, and stay, there.

This point has been empirically demonstrated, among those people who are at the other end of the spectrum of social privilege, by W. Lee Hansen and his colleagues in the United States. They examined the impact of education (defined as years of schooling) compared with other factors (learning, job training, job opportunities, family influences, and so on) on the earnings of 'low achievers'. So small was the relationship between length of schooling and earnings, for this group, that it led the authors to question the policy of encouraging the low achievers to remain at school. Just attending, they argue, is not enough – even assuming, given United States truancy rates, that these pupils do attend. *Learning* must take place; and that can be accomplished by out-of-school programmes. But equally important was their finding that these are, if anything, more dependent on 'ability, motivation, home encouragement' than is the quality/quantity of schooling.

On the face of it all, this emphasis on education reinforcing an individual's existing genetic and social capacities, seems inconsistent with the social and political role many would give to education as a means of equalizing opportunity in society, and of improving the life opportunities of the clever but underprivileged. It would seem to conflict directly with the life experience of our present Prime Minister, the Leader of the Opposition and the Head of the Civil Service – three people who could be case illustrations for Richard Hoggart's 'scholarship boy' or Dennis Potter's 'glittering coffin'. Such highly publicized examples seem to illustrate the power of education in dramatically creating opportunities for personal mobility. But how frequent is this sort of mobility? And how general are the experiences these examples would seem to exemplify?

Nearly two decades ago, C. Arnold Anderson re-worked David Glass's social mobility data, and he showed how easy and misguided it was to assume that education was achieving the objective of equalizing opportunity in society. Anderson demonstrated that a surprising number of people who had experienced a prolonged education were *downwardly* socially mobile, and a large number of less well-educated people achieved upward social mobility. He concluded there were too many of these 'deviant' cases for us to accept empirically the assumption of a close correlation between education and social mobility.

He went on to argue that the hypothesis that education, at any rate in Britain, was unrelated to mobility, explained as much of the observed relationship between level and type of education and future career as did the positive hypothesis that is normally assumed. He gave reasons why there was this lack of relationship. The existence in Britain of the private sector, giving education to an economically privileged, but intellectually impoverished, minority was one reason. Over and above this, he, too, underlined the facts that performance in work is dependent on a more varied, and different, set of talents than those developed and valued within the educational system; that education has multiple functions, and that preparation for a job is only one of them.

At best, these results question the capacity of the educational system to make really profound differences in a person's life chances, compared with his social origin and his genetic inheritance. At worst, it suggests that a great deal of what goes on in school (though justified, and perhaps justifiable, in 'educational' terms) has little or no relevance to the marketplace. Skills that are required to perform effectively at work are not merely an extension of school and schooling, but are perhaps qualitatively different from them. This does not undermine the hard workers at school/hard workers at work hypothesis. It simply indicates there are those who will work hard at *whatever* they are 'set' to do, whether it is useful or not.

Obviously one academic article does not make a truth. During the 20 years since Anderson published his article, we have seen (but not necessarily learnt) much. Two decades of explicit social and educational policy, not only in this country but in many industrial societies, have indicated how difficult it is to narrow social inequalities through educational policy and practice. The recent OECD review of world educational growth produced a number of statistics which showed (a) considerable growth in educational expenditure throughout all the affluent parts of the world, and considerable enlargements in enrolments;

and (b), parallel with this, the persistence of inequalities in school and in college participation and performance, despite policies designed to reduce or eliminate them.

It is tempting to see this as the result of what one might term gesture policies – policies designed to placate, but not change. But the results were common to types of political systems which were too widely different for one to accept this explanation. More realistically, one could argue that educational policies have not been potent enough, in either quality or quantity, to bring to put effective countervailing pressures onto the social differences that exist in society. It is possible, too, that the nature of these social differences is such that the room for manoeuvre, and the impact, of educational policy may be severely prescribed, whatever the resources.

There is another relevant point on mobility and education: just what sort of person becomes socially mobile? Information on the volume of mobility in contemporary society is not difficult to obtain; and increasing attention is being paid to the psychological correlates of mobility (the work of D. C. McClelland on the 'achievement factor' is an obvious example). But the illustration I want to give, in this present context, is J. W. B. Douglas's finding that the working class child who won selection to grammar school may well have come from the 'submerged' middle class. Either his father or more likely mother had been downwardly mobile. Looking back a generation suggests that many of the working class pupils in selective schools may come from families that were, till recently, members of the middle class.

A parallel example was noticed by Floud and Halsey in their classic study of educational opportunity. They found that children whose mother had 'married down' had far higher chances of obtaining a selective place than contemporaries whose parents both come from working class backgrounds, or who had broadly similar working class jobs before marriage. Social influences operate through time, to further limit the impact of contemporary attempts at social reform, and the intervening influence may well be what Geoffrey Hawthorn, in 'Family Background', refers to as maternal style and maternal power.

This interpretation would be consistent not merely with the type of findings arrived at by Anderson and the OECD review, but also with the most striking example of an explicit effort to compensate youngsters, through education, for disadvantages in their home background – in other words, the current American programmes of 'compensatory' education. (The British Educational Priority Areas policy is similar to these.) With a depressing consistency, the experience of the United States over the past five years has shown how ephemeral has been the impact of frequently well-financed, well-intended and intellectually well-designed programmes, aiming to improve the conditions of the disadvantaged through the educational system.

The problems of the disadvantaged are chronic and endemic, and the experience of these American efforts show how limited is the effectiveness of current intervention programmes. Similar conclusions are likely to come, in a diluted form, from our own more limited efforts under the EPA programme. We are ignorant, in fact, about the consequences of prolonged underprivilege (i.e. the social and psychological consequences of being disadvantaged). It is hardly surprising, therefore, that we are equally ignorant about effective strategies for meeting these problems within the orbit of the educational system. In a sense, the lesson learnt should be one of educational modesty. The tool we have is relatively weak, and the tasks we are trying to handle are long-lasting and deep-seated.

Obviously, this is not to deny that education has a significant impact on the prospects of some individuals. Everybody could make his own list of people he knows who have made changes in life through education. The tenth birthday of *Private Eye* in 1971, emphasising that magazine's Shrewsbury School and Oxford parentage, also re-emphasized the way in which school and university can open doors, channel talents and limit our circle of contacts. I am not trying to argue that such influences do not exist. I am saying that they tell us little about the general impact of education on our social structure, and about the working of education within it. Perhaps school and university can, in certain examples, exercise a profound and direct influence on an individual's future; but, compared with other forces in our society, its influence on most people's life-chances is limited.

An unusual example of this is the comparison that McQuail made of the influence of public school and state grammar school education on young people's political attitudes. His conclusion was notably similar to the one I have been arguing: public school education did not produce any 'striking' effects on the political attitudes of its pupils. Further, any differences in attitude between public school and grammar school pupils 'could as well be explained by differences of social background' as by differences in school experience. Admittedly, this was a study of the educationally privileged and the super-privileged; but it does more than support the argument that little or no difference could be found in political attitudes between the two groups. Equally important is the implication that even so total, so all-embracing, an institution as an English boarding school did little to diminish the influence of the family.

So far, I've tried to suggest that we can exaggerate the impact of education both on an individual's earning power and in improving an individual's life chances. But what

about the education system's more direct task of instruct-
ing youngsters in the three Rs – in other words, school
achievement in basic skills? From the sort of education
an individual has received, can we tell much about his
levels of literacy or numeracy?

The obvious answer is Yes. After all, young people leave
school with the public badges of their success (in Britain,
the Certificate of Secondary Education, GCE ordinary or
advanced levels). These tell us a good deal about what they
have achieved. Nationally, we take considerable pride in
both the increase in the numbers of pupils leaving school
who have passed public examinations, and in the improvements in general levels of literacy as shown by most succes-
sive Department of Education and Science reading surveys.
But my question is about the contribution of schooling as
such to these improvements, compared with the influences
of factors outside the school. It is impossible completely to
answer this. All I can do is give some empirical illustrations
that suggest that the influence of school is less than total.

Perhaps the most striking illustrations of the limited
impact of schooling (and school resources) compared with
extra-school factors are the studies of class size and reading attainment in primary schools. A study on Inner London Education Authority schools suggested that, at best,
class size was unrelated to the reading attainment of eight
to nine year olds. By contrast, children who came from
interested, supportive and stimulating homes had reading
ages of a year and a half above their age, social and ethnic
peers who came from unsupportive and uninterested home
backgrounds. It is wrong to deduce from this that schooling (or educational resources) has no impact: merely that
its impact is limited. A further study by the ILEA provides
another illustration of this: it was an inquiry into the
educational attainment of immigrants (especially West
Indians) in primary schools. The interesting point in this

context was that length of schooling, not length of residence, in this country was the important determinant of performance. West Indian pupils born here performed at the same level as those arriving before five; and both groups performed significantly better than pupils arriving in this country during the course of primary schooling. In a sense this is the measure of achievement of the school system: however, even with full United Kingdom schooling the performance of West Indians at age eleven was not as good as their indigenous class mates. For example, the indigenous had twice as many good performers as long-stay immigrants. This provides some measure of the inability of the school system, in the short run, to eliminate or compensate for social disadvantages.

Another illustration comes from the Plowden report on primary schools and is the much publicized 'weighting' which is given there to the various influences on a pupil's school progress. The measures of basic skill were numeracy and literacy, and they were used as general measures of performance. The analysis set out to give precision to the impact of home and other influences on a pupil. The findings are too well-known to require detailed repetition here; but the factor that helped explain most of the variance in pupils' school performance was parental interest. Neither the analysis nor this finding has gone uncriticized. Many are sceptical about the criteria of performance used; others question the information collected about parental interest and some of the actual techniques of analysis that were adopted. However, it is agreed that the broad findings stand – namely, the salient importance of extra-school influences on school performance.

This agreement is general, partly because it is consistent with the findings of other research workers like J. W. B. Douglas, in his year-by-year study of a large group of children from birth onwards. And the central finding has recently been confirmed by a follow-up investigation of the Plowden survey. Four years after the original survey, Peaker re-tested the same youngsters (on English, arithmetic and a non-verbal intelligence test), and he found the importance of home factors on performance still to be striking. He says, for example, that the influence of teaching on performance is about one third that of home circumstances. Put another way, the difference between the best and the worst teachers is never as great as the difference between intellectually rich and intellectually impoverished homes.

If this finding is correct, it indicates that excellent teachers can only compete to a limited extent with unsupportive homes. Perhaps, more encouragingly, poor teaching does not destroy the supportive influence of a literate and encouraging home. But Peaker is suitably guarded about this particular finding. The difficulty of getting valid measures of teaching performance is, he suggests, one reason for the apparent lack of impact of teaching. Furthermore, the difference between a good home and a bad one is far greater than the difference between good and bad teaching. Put simply, we would not tolerate such very bad schools, because they are in the public eye, in a way that homes are not. Peaker's main conclusion, like Plowden's, is that the major factors related to current levels of school achievement are parental circumstances, attitudes and practices. He concludes: 'The pattern in secondary schools is largely determined in the junior school, which in turn depends on the pattern in the earliest years.' His policy conclusion is the obvious one (which was once recognized by the Jesuits generations ago): the lasting importance of influences on children in their earliest years, and the need to provide different influences through nursery schools.

Similar general conclusions emerge from the Coleman

report on *The Equality of Educational Opportunity* in the United States. The empirical problem was different – explaining the variation in the performance of blacks compared with whites, or poor whites compared with rich whites, and trying to relate these variations to factors inside and outside the school. Things like the quality of the curriculum, the existence of special programmes for particular groups, and the social and ethnic composition of the classroom, were related to the performance of underprivileged groups. Again, it is the main finding that is worth repeating. What most closely correlated with variations in performance was not the obvious educational factors (the numbers and quality of teachers, or the standard of the library, or special programmes). It was the ethnic and social composition of the classroom. The more mixed it became (i.e. the higher the proportion of advantaged pupils), the better the performance of the underprivileged.

One final set of examples on the impact of educational change is relevant – namely, the effect of changes in teaching method and classroom organization. Recently, Warburton and Southgate have evaluated the new methods of teaching reading; and J. Barker Lunn has studied the effects of streaming of school performances. Both of these studies did much to destroy people's scepticism about certain aspects of the innovation in question (for example: are pupils confused by the transition from ITA to traditional orthography; or do clever pupils suffer by being taught in mixed ability groups?). However, the common finding, in my judgement, was how small were the differences that the inquiries found. On the whole, both studies came out with results favouring the innovations (i.e. ITA and unstreaming); but the differences between traditional and new practices, although consistent, tended to be small. This serves to reinforce my argument – that the contribution that education and educational change makes is small, because the freedom for manoeuvre is severely prescribed by other forces.

The Plowden and Coleman findings are in detail different, but in principle they reinforce each other and lead to the same conclusion about education and its role both on a general social level and in its impact on individuals. The empirical illustrations, in the case of Plowden, were the attitudes of parents; in Coleman the social and ethnic background of pupils. But the common element is, if I may rub the point in, the extent to which factors in the wider social structure curtail and limit the impact of the educational system, and its staff and resources.

Much as we might like education to be a powerful force for individual and/or social change, it is its impotency which is the more striking. Mark Twain suggested that 'soap and education are not as sudden as a massacre, but they are more deadly in the long run.' Can we wait for the long run? Or is there any way of making education the crucial variable it is commonly thought to be? For this, we shall need to do some hard re-thinking, based on an unglamorous appraisal of the realities. And to achieve any significant impacts, we shall need both more resources and greater flexibility in deploying them.

10 Leonard England and Wendy Grosse
Consumption

In mid-1971, extracts from a new survey by Professor Peter Townsend were published in the *Guardian*. They included case histories of three people said to be close to the poverty line. In one of them, a major item of expenditure was a hair-do; in another, a very expensive present for a child. In subsequent correspondence, *Guardian* readers (nearly half of them are reported to be in social class AB – i.e. probably earning over £2000 a year) argued that nobody could be regarded as all that poor if they had money to spend on non-essentials of such a kind.

The current relevance of this is not the nature of poverty. It is the assumption of an almost direct correlation not merely between the amount of income and the *amount* of expenditure, but between the amount of income and the *type* of expenditure. As income falls, more and more items must be discarded until the wretched pauper is allowed expenditure on nothing but food, housing and clothing. And hair-dressing obviously must count as a service rather than as clothing.

Clearly, there is enough truth in this to account for its wide acceptance as a theory. At subsistence level, it must be true that most money must be spent on a roof to one's head, something to wear, and something to eat. And presumably, at the other end of the scale, among multi-millionaires, it must be true that there is a limit to what can be spent on 'consumption', in that there is a finite amount of money which could be used for these basics and money must be left over for 'saving'. Except at the two extremes, however, it is impossible to divide expenditure into exclusive categories of 'essentials' and 'luxuries'. Almost all of us are given some choice in the way we spend, or the way we save, what we receive.

To say that we choose what we spend is perhaps slightly misleading, for many of the decisions affecting our consumption are not taken in these terms. If we have already decided to have (or have found ourselves with) six children, then we have six mouths to feed, and must in consequence spend more on food and clothing than somebody who has no children. If we have an invalid mother to look after, then we probably need to spend more on heating and on medicines. And so on. Thus, part of our expenditure pattern depends on the circumstances of our life over which we have no control, or else is caused by decisions quite unrelated to consumption patterns. But on top of this there are a further series of items over which we have far greater influence. For example, people in manual classes (C2, D, E) earn, on average, 66 per cent of the income of those in the managerial (A, B, C1) classes. Yet they spend more per head (absolutely not relatively) on tobacco. They find this money not by cutting down on the 'essentials', but by reducing on transport, travel and, above all, on services. They do-it-themselves, in other words, rather than use other people. So they are able to spend on what they *want* to spend.

Spending, in this context, must include various forms of saving. For some calculations in relation to expenditure surveys, a distinction is made between expenditure and 'balance', the latter generally assumed to be equivalent to saving. The distinction is often a very fine one; and, almost certainly, it is one not consciously used by the average household. But it is clearly correct, technically, that those who rent their house are *spending* money, while those who are paying off a mortgage are *saving* through one of a number of forms open to them. Many methods of saving can also be seen as investments. But each decision of this kind, whether made perforce or willingly, has an effect on expenditure patterns.

Imagine two families, A and B, with the same income, the same family composition, the same age grouping among its adults; but with different life patterns beyond that. Table 1 shows this:

Table 1 *How Families Differ*

family	A	B
annual income from all sources	£n	£n
age of head of household	mid-forties	mid-forties
family composition	wife and two children	wife and two children
travel to work	works on a farm, no journey to work	lives in outer suburb; heavy transport burden
home	lives in tied house	buying house on mortgage
children	left home and married	family to feed and clothe
wife	wife works	wife looks after family
leisure	odd jobs and television	interests involve purchase of technical equipment and books

A detailed pattern of expenditure from these two families would show very little in common. Family A would be spending markedly less on food, on transport and on rent. Even if both were spending the same amount on clothes, family A would be involved in more luxury spending, while family B would be concerned with the essential clothing for growing children. Family B would reserve money for 'leisure' (books, records, photography) at a scale which would amaze family A.

These patterns of expenditure are being influenced in these cases by a whole series of variables other than income – for we have assumed this to be constant. Some of these variables are fairly obvious, such as the occupation of the head of household and the area in which the family lives. But equally important are life cycle and life style. Even though the heads of the household may be of the same age, their family responsibilities are very different; and the burdens of bringing up the family which affect family B at the moment are those which family A had passed through earlier, when their other commitments were very different.

Life *cycles* are closely related to age. But life *styles* are not; and clearly, though the leisure interests of family B may reflect education, expenditure on leisure activities relates very much to personality and interests. It is true, in turn, that these may be related to where one lives or what one does for a living; but the relationships are not automatically clear. Thus, the docker and the bus driver, who need to be at their job very early in the morning, are likely to want to live near their work. Probably for that reason they are restricted to a comparatively small house even if their earnings might allow them to move to a larger one. In consequence, they have more 'free' money to spend on other items of leisure, whether drink, or cars, or football, or holidays on the Costa Brava. (The farm labourer is an instructive contrast: he, too, needs to live near his job, for similar reasons; but his earnings give him little option as to house size, and he has little 'free' money.)

The enthusiast, whether his interest is in promenade concerts or banger racing, will spend a larger proportion of his income on items which are very different, but which are never 'essential' spending. The do-it-yourself fanatic may well ultimately be saving, by dramatically improving the value of his house; but his hobby is costing him money at present, which in turn affects his consumption of other goods.

Table 2 *Expenditure Classed by Population Groups: Second Group Shown as % of First*

	occupation		household composition		urban/rural		region	
	managerial	manual	1 man, 1 woman, 1 child	1 man, 1 woman, 3 + children	Greater London	rural areas	Greater London	Scotland
housing	100	63	100	109	100	66	100	60
fuel, light, power	100	82	100	119	100	101	100	105
food	100	90	100	133	100	94	100	96
alcoholic drink	100	95	100	109	100	84	100	105
tobacco	100	135	100	121	100	82	100	109
clothing and footwear	100	68	100	115	100	78	100	86
durables	100	68	100	93	100	83	100	75
other goods	100	72	100	112	100	89	100	77
transport and vehicles	100	59	100	84	100	116	100	78
services	100	47	100	113	100	78	100	72
miscellaneous	100	84	100	241	100	77	100	104
total expenditure	100	73	100	113	100	88	100	84
total 'balance'	100	48	100	92	100	83	100	77
total income	100	66	100	109	100	87	100	82

Source: recalculated from Family Expenditure Survey, 1970

The working wife provides a further example. The fact that she works is often *basically* to add to the family income. But, in a great many cases, she may work primarily to earn money for special luxuries either for herself or for the family. And in certain cases the money may be entirely irrelevant – she may even do voluntary work – for her the central need will be interest. But whatever her income, her expenditure patterns will be quite different from those of next-door neighbours who stay at home. She will buy far more convenience foods, even if they are more expensive, because she will have less time for the family meal – the expense even of the most dramatic of these, like frozen chips, may be worthwhile. She is more likely to have 'working' or 'office' clothes, less likely to make her own or those of the rest of the family; and so on.

Table 2, drawn from the Family Expenditure Survey, indicates how families in widely different occupation groups, with different household compositions, and in different administrative areas and regions, vary in their purchasing patterns. In all cases, the age of the head of the household is held roughly constant at between 40 and 50 years.

We noted earlier that manual workers spend 35 per cent more than white-collar workers on tobacco, but 53 per cent less on services. There are few other variations as great as this but it is noticeable that though country dwellers earn 13 per cent less than the inhabitants of London, they spend 16 per cent more on transport and vehicles. (It is quite right for Michael Chisholm to point out, in his chapter on 'Location', that to live in the country one increasingly needs to be well-off.) Scots – again compared to the Greater Londoners – have 18 per cent less income, but they spend 9 per cent more on tobacco and 5 per cent more on fuel, lighting and power – also more on alcohol – compensated by their spending much less on housing.

These are differences in expenditure emerging from general groupings. They can be broken down to show detailed patterns of use; but perhaps we should, first, be clear that 'consumption', or 'use', is not entirely the same as 'expenditure'. The heavy 'consumer' of television is not spending any more than the light 'consumer', apart from a marginal addition on electricity. The heavy 'user' of libraries is spending no more on his reading than the light 'user'. And this observation probably applies to many other areas. There are further pitfalls: use of lipstick, for example, is apparently not correlated with expenditure, because middle-aged women buy fewer lipsticks, and go on using them until they are finished; younger women, on the other hand, are more likely to buy more lipsticks and throw them away half-used.

'Use profiles' can be very revealing. Where the unit-cost is high (cars, for example, or private doctors), there is a close link between expenditure and income. But often there are puzzles. If we could have assumed that spending on holidays would be higher in the middle class, and among younger people, would we also have expected another marked peak among people between 45 to 54 (when children have left home?) and in the west midlands but not in the east midlands? It may be obvious that bikinis are more likely to be bought in the south of England than in the north; but is it equally obvious that the same applies to mohair coats and aluminium garden chairs? Yorkshire housewives spend very little on asparagus. This may be predictable, but is it also predictable that they buy fewer umbrellas? Those who sometimes spend money on laxatives are not merely older (probably to be expected) but also middle class (why?). But those who spend *heavily* on laxatives come from all age groups and all class groups proportionately. People who live in the country are proportionately more likely to cook by gas. The buying of chocolate bars is slanted toward women; but men are equally likely to buy chocolate assortments.

The list is almost endless and differences can be noted in brands as well as in general product-fields. If a house-wife is known to spend on one brand of luncheon meat rather than another, we can predict something about the part of the country in which she lives. If her husband tends to buy one motor oil rather than another, we can tell something about his age. If together they buy one brand of tea rather than another at much the same price, we can tell something about their class.

The Family Expenditure Survey table shows that the 'balance' left to various groups differs considerably. But this 'balance' contains many different ingredients, ranging from tax and insurance contributions to the purchase of savings certificates. A more specialised survey on savings can tell us more detail. Almost equal proportions of the population, for example, save heavily (i.e. over £1000 in their lifetime), through building societies and through other sources. Building society savers, however, are much more likely to be over 55 years old and much more likely to be men. Sex differences in methods of saving are exten-sive. Despite the greater longevity of women, men, who account for only 48 per cent of the British population, hold 59 per cent of all the money invested. Yet women outnumber men investors in each method of government saving – though the only form for which they account for the greater part of the funds invested is the Post Office Savings Bank. Again, would one have guessed that, in num-bers, there are a great many more women than men with bank deposit accounts?

Take holidays. Some variations occur, as we have seen, by age and by region. But there are many other variations as well. Before the troubles, at least, those who went to Northern Ireland for a holiday spent 25 per cent more on holidays annually than those who stayed in England, even after discounting the fare. Yet the composition of these visitors shows *fewer* people in the higher income-brackets than for those visiting any area in England. This is another indication of the lack of exact correlation between income and expenditure.

Take another region. If we know that a family has been to Scotland for a holiday, we also know that they are more likely than average :

To come from Scotland itself, or the north of England, or from London; and if the Highlands are in question, very much more likely to come from the London area.

To belong to the professional and managerial classes, and to have above-average income.

To be middle-aged.

To take much longer holidays 'in one piece' than those holidaying in other areas within Britain, and to spend more on hotels and boarding houses.

To travel more by train (except those going to the Highlands).

Or take housing. The FES table shows an overall pattern; again, more detailed research reveals great variations within the pattern. One of the vital factors in buying a house is one's ability to find the initial deposit. Single-person households, while spending less on their houses (when they own them at all), have to find a higher percentage for the deposit (32 per cent of the value when bought, as against 21 per cent for households with three or more in the family). House purchasers in Scotland are asked to pay more (27 per cent of the value) than those in the Greater London area (at 25 per cent, the deposit proportion is lower here than anywhere else). Working-class people have to find a higher proportion than middle-class people.

Or take personal expenditure on welfare services. Those who do pay for some, at least, of their children to be educated are younger than most parents; those who contribute to private health services are older than the general population. But we know, too, that if a person pays for either education or health over and beyond state contributions, he is more likely to live in the south of England than in the north (though private education is also popular in Scotland). And paying for schooling is not the middle-class prerogative which might have been expected. Almost half of those whose children are not being educated in state schools come from the manual (C2DE) class. This may be another example of income not being directly related to expenditure.

The more detail we have of consumption/expenditure, the more we know about the individual. But it is much more difficult to pin this down than some of the other variables covered in this book. A survey researcher can (with very few exceptions) assess the sex of a respondent, or know in what region he is living, without asking anything at all; while a single question demanding a single-word answer will give a respondent's age, marital status, and so on.

Even the more complex issues like income or religion yield data to a comparatively few questions, with at least sufficient accuracy for general conclusions to be drawn about a wide range of characteristics. With consumption, there are no neat, mutually exclusive groupings. We can never talk meaningfully about 'high' or 'low' consumptions, and divide people into groups in this way.

We can study people as consumers with rather more confidence, however, once we know how much they spend on different key items. But this takes a good deal of time and effort. The complexity of collection means that such data are rarely available *from the same survey* in more than one expenditure field. We are rarely, for example, able to relate *methods* of saving with *methods* of spending on education or health, and see whether age or region, for example, affects the combined pattern. But there are very few aspects of consumption or expenditure on which no information at all can be collected after a reasonable amount of ferreting – of value, provided that we know details not only of sample but also of timing. It is probable that expenditure patterns change with rather more speed than most of the other variables considered in this series.

A colour television set in 1970 might have ranked its owner as middle class and probably middle-aged; but this was likely to be far less true in 1971; and probably not true at all in 1972. The use of instant sauces or outboard motor boats could have reflected quite a different profile two years ago than today; while ownership of refrigerators has risen from 7 per cent to 56 per cent of the population in a matter of 13 years (far larger than the rise in real income could allow us to expect).

The greater the degree of detail available, the greater the sensitivity to change. Overall changes are much lower : expenditure on food, expressed as a percentage of total available income, has changed only by 3 per cent in seven years and on clothing by 1 per cent. But this fails to reflect the size of changes that are going on within the total concept.

For example, the value of tea expressed as a percentage of all beverages bought has dropped by 9 per cent within the last seven years. In other fields, there are even more remarkable variations in expenditure patterns. To take one extreme : whereas in the course of the last seven years the average income has gone up by about half, the amount spent on maintaining and running motor vehicles has practically doubled. There are similar variations in many

specific groups But the information could be very misleading if out-of-date data were used.

Technological developments and the increased chance
of leisure (even if one chooses to work overtime in it)
will almost certainly speed up opportunities to spend in
different ways. Consumption patterns will continue to
fragment. They will, increasingly, provide data on the individual as an *individual*, rather than as a member of a
predetermining social *group*.

11 Julius Gould
Nationality and Ethnicity

Nationality and 'ethnicity' are dimensions of great subtlety and importance. Knowledge of the simple ethnic or national 'facts' about an individual is not of itself very revealing or rewarding. To know of someone that he is, say, an American Jew or a British-resident West Indian is clearly to learn *something* about his national or ethnic position – to locate him *somewhere* on the social map. And, for certain very simple purposes of classification, this may be enough. But an individual's national or ethnic 'identity' has a group aspect. How does the American Jew relate to other Jews? Is he religious or not? Does he live in Georgia; or in New York, where there are more Jews to whom to relate and where the ethnic structures, both white and black, are also very different from those found in Georgia? Does he, and in what ways, relate to Israel, a far-off land whose fortunes could affect his own? And so on. Does the black West Indian live in Camden Town, in the north London interstices of Irish and Cypriot settlements (and of 'English' professionals, newer arrivals still, busy doing up old houses); or is he, say, in Nottingham, where, he may feel, only the Poles seem to have preceded him? Is he young or old; a labourer or a doctor? Does he intend to stay in Britain? Does he know precisely what he intends? And, once more, so on. And, in both these examples, does the individual find himself, in general, in a situation of acceptance or rejection by the wider society? And what defences, including group solidarity, does our individual have against rejection, whether social, economic or political?

To raise these questions is not to answer them. The only

scientific answers must come from more detailed inquiry and observation. Such questions do, however, bring out the need to abandon global stereotypes, whether of nationality or ethnicity – especially when these have been influenced, however tacitly, by assumptions about racial distinctiveness. There are notorious difficulties in the doctrines that 'nations' are 'races', or that 'races' can become pure 'nations'. There is no scientifically satisfying evidence that there are fixed racial types, or that cultural attributes are determined by inborn differences. On these, and related issues, there is room for further investigation. But ethnicity, race or nationality are perceived by men as social categories. The genetic source is extremely obscure and may be of doubtful relevance. In the scientific debates on environment versus heredity, a verdict of Not Proven seems often the most prudent. For whatever the genetic facts, they would not, at any rate in the short run, destroy the symbolic or moral meanings which men give to national or ethnic divisions.

'Ethnic' is often used where 'racial' seems a narrow or discredited term. Thus, in the United Kingdom, the Social Science Research Council's Race Relations Research Unit was re-named 'Research Unit on Ethnic Relations.' This, correctly, opens up a new, wider and more diverse set of symbolic meanings – and, of course, the possibility that these meanings may be combined and recombined in different ways.

So far as ethnic groups or 'social' (as distinct from 'biological') races are concerned, these meanings are the deposit of social history. They are the result of majority or minority status, and of positions of superiority or inferiority, within a power system.

In his useful appraisal of the British scene, Ernest Krausz pinpoints this concern with *minority* status and it is on 'minorities' that most ethnic studies have understandably focussed. But he is right to stress, following Ruth Glass, that it is the status of being outsiders on the 'margin' that attracts scientific as well as moral attention. 'It is this qualitative aspect rather than the quantitative fact of being few in number that really matters.'

Ethnicity has at least two levels, in all societies. On one level, among some of the people some of the time, these social realities are correctly and sensitively perceived; on another, they are distorted by self-serving stereotypes, by ritualized ways of perceiving one's partners in social inter-action.

Stereotypes are not confined to ethnic situations. They 'help' to define the perceived social importance of age and sex and class. But, despite what Women's Liberationists may feel, they have had the most serious impact in the area of nationality and ethnicity. Their content has varied from the marginally false to the hate-laden and the paranoid. Whatever the 'correct' definition of a national or ethnic group may be, the collectives to which the terms relate have aroused the most powerful of sentiments; and in the service of those collectives, men have displayed both great nobility and extreme depravity.

This is an area full not only of unclear, shifting defini-tions, but also of linguistic nuances and traps. For curious reasons, the British have been much less vocal than other 'nations' about the finer points of national identity. Less happier lands – notably the Americans – have seemed ob-sessed both with the creation of a national order at the political level and with fundamental questions of identity. Of course, in the American case – unlike the Canadian or Australian cases – there was a conscious concern with the philosophy, and limited practice, of the 'melting pot'. It was supposed that earlier national and ethnic character-istics would be effectively moulded by a common set of 'American' experiences. It would be wrong to suppose that the melting pot was just a convenient social myth. But its effectiveness was no more than partial even among American white 'ethnics', and it was tragically limited so far as black Americans were concerned.

The British, though their population has long been more mixed than they proclaimed, never developed so explicit a philosophy. They treated the problems of those on the margins of the majority society, whether French Huguenots or German Jews, with a general benign neglect. To the question, 'What is an American?' there used to be no British counterpart. (And one may feel that its absence, however convenient, closed British eyes to certain issues of social science for far too long.) But times have changed. With the coming of coloured immigrants to Britain in large numbers, new issues of nationality – some real, some spurious – have emerged.

British nationality is an 'ascribed' status for most Britons – i.e. a datum that one cannot choose. But the formal criteria have been shifted and modified by the Commonwealth Immigrants Act, 1971. No reader of the recent parliamentary debates on 'patriality' – the new attempt to define British nationality – could mistake the changed atmosphere. Yet there have always been ambiguities on a plane below the legal forms. To be British, and to have United Kingdom citizenship, is one thing. But to be English is quite another. The Jews in Britain – a small, well-treated ethnic group – have long felt this ambiguity. The second- and the third-generation Jew, even his naturalized ex-Russian or ex-German father, is clearly British. But can he see himself, and also be seen by others, as English?

Now, for many Jews, this has not been overtly or consistently troublesome. But the distinction between being British and being English, is a real one; and in some ways, it has affected Jewish 'presentation of the self' in Britain. Unlike America, Britain does not give any structural supremacy to white Anglo-Saxon Protestantism; but 'Englishry' is, in some measure, a distinct cultural pattern, from which outsiders, even British 'nationals', can feel, and be made to feel, selectively excluded. It is often a tacit major premise, but at times it can become almost whimsically articulate. During the revivals of Welsh and Scots nationalism in the late 1960s, Englishmen were heard to say, half-seriously, that they, too, should strive for autonomy via regional devolution.

The motifs of Englishness derive from diffuse cultural attributes *within* the national context, and they are liable to become more specific in times of change and stress. (War, for example, makes many meanings explicit: witness the nuances in the work of Evelyn Waugh or Noel Coward.) But, over and above such quasi-ethnic motifs, there are bound to be new and shifting sources of national identity, even for a nation which believes itself exempt. Being British is bound to imply certain historically grounded perceptions, and misperceptions, of others – of other nations with whom we have been at war, or over whom (how long ago it seems . . .) we have exercised imperial control. Indeed, the state of mind of a post-imperial power like Britain is inevitably coloured – if I may be allowed the word – in its perception of aliens, whether European, African or Asian, by its recollection of past glories.

It will be recalled that for the Institute of Race Relations' volume, *Colour and Citizenship*, Mark Abrams surveyed attitudes held by respondents in five British boroughs about the 'superiority' of the British over people in other parts of the globe. Not surprisingly, about a third of the respondents felt the British were 'definitely superior' to Africans, and another third felt that the British were 'superior to some extent'. Somewhat similar reactions to Asians were reported; and so were 'reduced' (but still interesting) reserves of superiority towards Europeans and

Americans. Too much should not be made of such data, given the usual problems of questionnaire semantics. But they confirm what I would argue for on quite general grounds. The logic of national distinctiveness seems to entail this kind of acute, but graded, sense of superiority.

Great convulsions in national identity often occur when this sense of superiority conflicts with current reality. It can have traumatic outcomes. France, for example, in its Algerian war, openly lived through such a trauma, at the end of a long history of defeat and withdrawal in three continents. It came to transcend it through the mystiques of Gaullism and technocracy. Britain, I have always felt, suppressed its analogous trauma – partly because it yielded more gracefully to the winds of imperial change. But it is unlikely that so long and so remarkable an imperial past can disappear without leaving some psychological scars; and I think the suppression has had consequences for British politics and culture which have gone largely unexamined. The coming of coloured immigrants (to meet Britain's 'shortages' of labour – a culturally acceptable definition of the situation) may well have sparked off some potentially pathological traits, which have to be recognized before they can be overcome. Here Enoch Powell may have proved both a historical symbol and a catalyst. Traumatic unease, again, seems to have lain behind some of the debates on Britain's joining the European Common Market. On this issue, a reasonable concern over benefits and costs seemed to be fed at times, and in unusual places, by a vain of atavism and of nostalgia for an irrecoverable national past.

I shall not seek to define 'a nation'. The long history of such definitions shows how tentative and tortuous the effort can be. Given the variety of self-styled and recognized nations, no single or simple definition can contain all of them; still less explain either their origins or the course of their development. Yet such a 'national course' can be all-important. No one can say, for example, whether national identity in Israel would have been different if Israel had had a less martial history since 1948. But the possibility that it would have been different can still be entertained, and can enter into debate over the meaning of the new Jewish state.

One thing can, and must, be said about 'nationhood', because it appears to be of wide relevance. Clearly, a nation is a grouping whose institutions transcend local and regional ties: it is a politically crucial form of unity which rests upon, and limits, an inner diversity. This political pattern arose in Europe, and has been widely imitated and followed elsewhere. But the *form* of the unity, and the *content* of the diversities, are both highly variable. Contemporary Canada, Ireland, Britain and Nigeria are all nations. But in no two of these cases is there the same sense of national identity. In no two is there the same level, sense, or tone, of national consciousness. Again, America under Theodore Roosevelt and under Lyndon Johnson was imbued by comparable senses of national mission. But the world contexts of these missions were not the same.

These examples can be multiplied. They suggest, as one would expect, that while a man's nationality (except for such cases as dual nationality) can be 'coded' by a survey as simply as we can code his height or weight, there remains the question of what it means to him. Such meanings can only be extracted from a detailed picture of how the individual sees the world. This demands a study not only of how salient his nationality is to him personally, but of group relations considered in historical depth.

It could be argued, as it was by that keen observer, Ernest Renan, that, for a major human group to become a nation, it must share, over a specified period of time, a common heritage – 'a heritage of glory and grief to be shared,' common suffering, hopes and fears. Yet, like any general perspective, this one, too, must be returned to specific historical fact. The common experiences which Renan invoked can only become 'common' to a group if the group already has a prior capacity for securing community. Where such a capacity is missing, a common history or heritage will not weld the population into a nation with a structure of common institutions and sentiments. Witness the misfortunes of the Germans in Czechoslovakia, or the chaos in Northern Ireland. There are, naturally, explanations for this 'failure' to jell into nationhood. They always involve pressures which are both internal and external to the population concerned.

Much recent social science thinking on nationhood and the meaning of nationality has been sparked off by debates over modernization and nation-building. The resulting historical comparisons have brought in new material and have been most illuminating. For they have helped us to see in perspective the earlier western European movement towards national identity. And the nationhood of the latecomers, especially in the post-colonial period, is now seen to have its own special and complex contents. Within this wide, cross-historical context, writers such as Samuel Huntington and Reinhard Bendix have sought to make nationhood a core-criterion for modernity.

In a famous paper, Huntington, for example, distinguishes modern from earlier polities in the light of three criteria: their success in rationalizing authority, in developing specialized agencies for performing new state functions, and in absorbing mass participation in politics. A nation – the prototypes being the post-feudal developments in Europe – involves, in the words of Huntington, the exercise of 'internal sovereignty' on the part of the government over regional and local ties. And the study of modernization is, in part, the study of how new states succeed, or fail, in exercising such internal sovereignty. For it is always an open historical and empirical issue whether it is easy, or even possible, to secure that minimum (but high) level of paramountcy for national, as distinct from other aspirations. Time may be needed to build up a sense of nationality.

Some entrenched groups may seek exemptions in the name of primordial symbols which they value more; other groups are too greedy to wait for the benefits that they have been promised. Elites and leaders may cajole or bully – before they, too, start to distrust one another. In the outcome, the periphery becomes too strong for the centre. Society becomes too strong for the nascent state.

In some new states, the issue of nationality and nation-building becomes interwoven with ethnic conflicts. It is no mere debating point to recall that ethnic discrimination occurs along a black-brown as well as along a black-white line of division. It has been the tragedy of countless thousands within the Indian groups in Kenya and Uganda that they have been such visible targets for economic envy and dispossession – the victims of a policy of Africanization against which there can be no protection. (A somewhat different, though perhaps deeper, tragedy – and in quite different circumstances – is that of the South African 'Coloureds'. There can be few populations more cross-pressured, and more exposed to a multiplicity of hates and spites from their black and white 'fellow citizens' . . .) But even where these ethnic problems do not arise, or are secondary in importance, the course of nation-building in such societies today cannot follow, or be expected to follow, the European path. As Gunnar Myrdal put it in 1968, in his *Asian Drama* : 'The fundamental reason is that an historical process that in Europe spans centuries is telescoped within a few centuries, and that the order of the happenings is deranged.'

It is not only among the 'new states' that ethnicity tears at the fabric of the nation. Group loyalties, based on real or supposed common origins and ties, are at the heart of ethnicity. Such loyalties hit the headlines from Canada as well as the United States; from Ireland and Belgium; even from within the predominantly Jewish population of Israel. Lines of ethnic division can coincide with lines of linguistic and religious schism. But the link between ethnicity and social class is the one which produces the deepest of cleavages. And when, as in the United States, we encounter a complex of colour, ethnicity and class, the mixture is at its most explosive. The Kerner Commission data published in 1968 on the American Negro, showed how, over nine years, the proportion of Negro families at middle and upper middle income levels had risen from 7 per cent to 28 per cent. There was a second broad income band which contained 41 per cent of Negro families – a rise, also over nine years, from 29 per cent.

At the bottom, however, 32 per cent of all Negro families were below the 'poverty line' – i.e. 'needing,' if not always receiving, welfare payments. It was small consolation to this group that, nine years before, the equivalent percentage had been just over twice as high. The group's reference point was, more likely, the *contemporary* fact that only 13 per cent of white families were below the poverty line. Moreover, of the black poor, more than two million people were the 'hard-core disadvantaged', living in inner-city areas and disproportionately afflicted with a whole range of social ills. Here is the 'underclass', for whom ethnicity means something very specially disabling. It is this underclass which frightens black and white Americans alike, for it is often forgotten that, though the American underclass is intolerably large, it constitutes but a tenth of the total American black population. One of the few encouraging signs in the American ethnic situation is the growth of moral and of political involvement by *some* of the black 'upper' groups in the fate of the urban dispossessed.

Two strands interweave in men's thinking about their ethnicity. First, they wish the freedom to maintain 'their' culture, to practise 'their' religion, or to preserve 'their' customs. And, second, they seek to enjoy the general rights of citizenship claimed by all others. The 'ethnic' wants his ethnicity to be both relevant and irrelevant. And social systems find it difficult to satisfy both of these wants. Coloured minorities claim that their colour itself is almost a dirty word. In many lands, they (as well as religious minorities) have been denied the basic status of equality, described by T. H. Marshall, in his classic discussion of citizenship, as 'a status bestowed on all those who are full members of the community'. Marshall showed that this basic formal status conflicted with, yet helped to abate, the sharp facts of class inequality. The welfare state was, in fact, among other things, a set of devices for class abatement and for national unification on new principles.

The tensions between ethnicity and nationality can be analysed in parallel to Marshall's analysis of class and citizenship. Ethnic diversity will not prove more tractable than class diversity. And the 'abatement' of ethnic inequalities, blending ethnicity into strengthened national frameworks, calls for institutional devices as novel as those of the welfare state. What they will be, none can foretell. They will result from the pressures of ethnicity, and from the 'revolt against inequality' of which Philip Mason has written in his *Patterns of Dominance*. And they will not be 'perfect' devices, purporting to solve stubborn problems by incantation or ideology.

It may seem naive to see grounds for hope among our present ethnic conflicts. But hope can, paradoxically, be drawn from the seemingly catastrophic collapse of much conventional wisdom on these matters. Many societies – notably the United States – have, in recent years, shown signs of *deepening* ethnicity – a dramatic change – in the self-estimation of *blackness*, as well as counterploys of white resentment and of sophisticated, if not always well-planned, concessions to the new mood. Though there are overtones of hysteria and fear, this new consciousness could prove a prelude to an eventual accommodation. It is a gamble with fate. The way in which an individual's nationality or ethnicity impinges on him is governed in part at least by his willingness to gamble. Heightened ethnicity brings ridiculous displays of racialistic self-regard. But displays like this among the disadvantaged may contain the grains of a new and valuable self-esteem. Those who do not esteem themselves (or who have been robbed of their self-esteem) cannot begin to esteem their fellow-men.

Being a member of an *ethnos*, or belonging to a national (or proto-national) community, makes very diverse claims upon the 'ethnic' or 'national' individual. Such an individual will come near to an ideal type (or stereotype?) of an embattled or embittered separateness when conditions like these are met: (a) the stronger his (or her) identification with the group; (b) the deeper that group's sense of being distinct and, most important, of being distinctively higher or lower than some other group; (c) the greater the sense (or reality) of deprivation, both absolute and relative, *or* the fear of loss of privilege.

Ethnicity seems, also, to have cumulative effects. When a man, through his ethnic ties, has limited access to one social sphere, this can 'cumulate' into other spheres and reinforce the initial limitation. But it would be wrong to claim that this must be universal. What is more, the individual, if not the group, is free to depart from the ideal type, to transcend his 'destiny'. In terms of his own personality, or in terms of other emergent group-forces, he may react selectively to the ethnic options. And what these options are cannot be deduced from any flat assertion of ethic identity. (For example, a Jew in Tsarist Russia could choose to become either a Bundist socialist *or* a Zionist.) Such options restrict, or expand, a man's ethnic or nationalist militancy. They make possible, or inhibit, trans-ethnic coalitions. Yet, like all that is social, they both arise from historical 'givens', and are endlessly re-shaped by human purpose, ambition and contrivance.

Interest in religion as a key variable has been a central feature of sociological analysis ever since it was studied intensively by the sociologists of the so-called classical period – roughly, 1890 to 1920. Max Weber undoubtedly contributed most to the exploration of the relationship between religious and other variables, especially in examining the relationship between religion and economic behaviour. In this latter respect he was, above all, interested in the differences between Roman Catholics and Protestants in their attitudes towards work and industrial enterprise. This was essential to Weber's almost life-long interest in the development of what he called the spirit of capitalism. On Weber's view, Protestantism, particularly in its Calvinistic forms, was a crucial factor in the spread of entrepreneurial modes of economic behaviour and organization.

Many sociologists have, historically, been interested in religious factors, on the presumption that, as these factors are cultural fundamentals – sources of 'ultimate meaning' – they must have a great deal of causal significance. However, it seems to be widely agreed that the present century – in particular, its last two decades – has been a time of secularization, and that this process is central to many modern societies. Yet this has the consequence of *heightening* social scientific interest in religion: it needs detailed study; and its social and psychological implications need to be assessed.

The methods of carrying out this evaluation have grown more sophisticated. But the quest for precision has brought about much confusion. As sociologists have become more conscious of the complex interplay between (say) religion, social class and political preference, they have had to enter caveats about what were thought to be fairly well-established generalizations.

For example, sociologists seemed by the end of the 1930s to have shown that religiosity was greatest among the higher social strata of industrial societies. Much of the evidence for this was based on membership of religious organizations. Since that time, students have come to feel that this is but one among a number of measures of religion. There is no consensus, however, on what should be regarded as the major indicators. Thus, any attempt to summarize findings must be frequently confounded by the fact that different analysts, including those who undertake public opinion surveys, use different ones. But nearly all inquiries into relationships between religion and other variables may be looked at in terms of two major kinds of *dimension*.

First, there are dimensions of a *social* kind. Under this heading come studies which concentrate on such things as church attendance and membership of religious organizations. Second, there is a broader category which can be called the *cultural* side. Here, two aspects get special attention: (a) the degree of commitment to beliefs of a religious kind; (b) devotional matters, like the saying of prayers. We call these 'cultural' because they deal with the cognitive content of religion – in contrast to the 'social side', which concerns the interactions between individuals gathered together in the name of religion. There are many sociologists who regard the cultural side as the more significant. But neither can be ignored, particularly since there is considerable variation among the members of modern societies about what *they* regard as being 'really religious' involves.

The firmness of the association between religion and other characteristics of an individual varies with different societies. In a tight, polarized situation like Northern Ireland, one can predict quite a lot about an individual simply by asking: 'With which religious group do you identify?' In the United States, too, with just a little more interviewing sophistication, one could quite safely make a number of predictions. This is not to say that the United States is similar to Northern Ireland in terms of the salience of religious factors. The United States is not polarized along religious lines. On the other hand, religion counts more in American life than in, for example, English life.

One's confidence about the American situation would be higher than in the English case for two main reasons. First, there is no established church, attracting a lot of highly 'nominal' adherents, in the United States. And though Protestants are in the majority, they are split into a large number of denominations. There is, however, a major cleavage between black Protestants and white Protestants; these two groups differ markedly both politically and economically. Second, and in close conjunction with this latter point, ethnic identity in America is closely bound up with religious identity. In the United States – as in Northern Ireland – it makes a great deal of sense to talk in terms of what Gerhard Lenski, in *The Religious Factor*, has called 'socio-religious membership.'

This can be measured in terms of the degree to which individuals are married to someone in the same group and have relatives and close friends drawn almost exclusively from it. Very nearly 70 per cent of people in England claim to have some kind of allegiance towards the Church of England. That percentage manifests, as a whole, characteristics similar to those of the overall population (in terms of sex ratio, age, occupational distribution, and so on). So one has only a small proportion of the population – around 25 per cent, or less – to which one can refer in order to discover something interestingly 'non-religious' about an individual, on the basis of knowing simply his denominational inclination. Since, in turn, about half of that minority group are Protestant Nonconformists, having much in common with Anglicans, one is left only with Jews and Roman Catholics of whom one can talk in terms of socio-religious groups in Lenski's sense. Both Jews and Catholics are, as groups, fairly tight-knit. Among Catholics, this is most true of those who are of Irish origin.

In the Detroit area, some ten years ago, Lenski found that, for no less than thirty-five dependent variables, people's socio-religious group membership was, on the whole, slightly more powerful than their social class. This finding has been a major focus of a debate about whether it is a *religious* factor, as opposed to *historical* experiences, which shapes the political, economic and social relationships of religious groups to their society.

Much of the debate has concerned Catholicism. Catholics in Britain tend to vote mainly for the Labour Party and, in America, for the Democratic candidates. This is partly because these Catholics are largely urban working class, partly because they are minority groups, and only in minor respects because of the belief system of Catholicism. Many American Catholics have conservative political attitudes, but they still favour the more left-wing party. Their 'left-wingness' is based on a desire to change the system in favour of their own form of conservatism. So the question still remains: is this a *religious* factor at work?

Bearing firmly in mind all the kinds of problem I have raised, we can, nevertheless, pin down some more detailed relationships between religion and two sets of individual characteristics: on the one hand, with characteristics that have to do with objective social circumstances (age, sex, class and marital status); and, on the other hand, with more attitudinal characteristics (politics, economic attitudes, race and sexual behaviour).

Age, first, then. People who are more intense in their religion are likely to be either in their mid-teens or over fifty. Many studies carried out in the 1950s and 1960s found that religion tends to be consciously chosen or rejected – as the case may be – at about the age of sixteen. There then is among those on the 'religious path' quite a rapid decline, until in the early thirties there begins a steady build-up until death. In Britain at least, however, regular church attendance as such tails off in the early-to-mid-sixties for all religious bodies, and particularly for Roman Catholics. One can never be sure that 'snapshot' studies reflect individuals' life-cycles. Some studies could be no more than analyses of age distribution at a particular point in time. But the evidence is fairly firm.

It has long been known that women tend to be more religious than men on almost every measure. The differences are significant in the social dimensions of religion, but they are at their greatest in the area of belief and, even more, devotionalism. There are variations among religious bodies, however. It is in sectarian Protestantism (for example, Christian Science and Christadelphianism) that one finds the greatest sex differences – i.e. the most women. The smallest differences are in more mainstream religious bodies like the Roman Catholic church. It is among Jews that religion seems to be most equally balanced. Indeed, some American studies show a definite tendency for Jewish men to be more religious than women.

Conventional explanations for women being more religious tend to hinge on the allegedly greater emotionalism of women and on their marginality to the 'moving forces' of complex societies. Quite regardless of the extent to which one or another variety of women's liberation ideology is having a marked effect on the self-identification of women in modern societies, it seems very likely that the more practical and 'mundane' changes in women's positions will attenuate some of these male/female differences in respect of religious behaviour patterns and beliefs.

An individual's marital status is obviously intertwined with both sexual category and age. But, even allowing for this, there is a disproportionately large number of single people among the religiously active (along both social and cultural dimensions). A large proportion of the highly religious are widows or widowers; and, as one would expect, these are particularly religious along the cultural dimensions (belief and devotion).

The situation is complicated, however – particularly if one defers to the idea that married people attend church less because of child responsibilities. There is some American evidence that couples with children are more likely to express 'much interest' in religion than childless couples are. In contrast, there is English evidence that many married individuals declaring themselves to be 'very religious' are childless. The relationship existing between religion and marital situation is a good example of the complex interplay between religious and non-religious factors.

Similar complexity arises in the relationship between religion and social class. On all the most publicly displayed measures of religion – mainly of the social kind – it is the middle classes who turn out to be the most religious. The self-consciously irreligious are also to be found here more often. But higher social strata are much more prone to be 'joiners'; lower down there is a less formal and frequently more *cultural* religious disposition. Emphasis on the social necessity of religion is clearly linked to the well-attested fact that people who see themselves as highly religious tend to be politically conservative. Some researchers – particularly those in America – have discovered that the people who go to church more regularly have less strong religious beliefs. The long-standing claim that the lower classes are without religion has, therefore, been challenged by contemporary sociologists.

Such challenges have to be set alongside poll data which suggest that, both in Britain and the United States, participation *and* belief are linked to class. The higher the individual socially, the greater his religious participation, *and* the more committed he or she is to, for example, belief in God. The critics of these data point to the significance of superstition and to what David Martin calls 'subterranean theologies'. The fact remains that, in terms of the conventional appurtenances of religion, the lower social strata, notably in Britain, have in modern history been a-religious.

The only important reservation in Britain is the fact that the working class is 'over-represented' in the Catholic church. In America, the situation is much less clear-cut: there is a clearer hierarchy of religious groups, which roughly matches the system of social stratification. In America, denominational switching is much more common; and a lot of that switching is contingent on movement on the 'status ladder'.

So far I have mainly discussed factors which, on the whole, condition how religious an individual is. In the case of politics, economic behaviour, sexual behaviour and racial attitudes, it is more a question of how these things are themselves shaped by religion.

Many studies of religion and economics, but by no means all of them, have confirmed the general outline of Weber's arguments about the differences between Roman Catholics and Protestants. On commitment to work, the importance of budgeting and saving, and belief in the worthwhileness and possibility of 'worldly' success, Protestants often score higher than Catholics. Little firm evidence exists about this in British society, however. American studies tend to find that these generalizations apply most to white Protestants and Jews; black Protestants have much in common with the Catholics. The general difference in economic beliefs and attitudes are reflected in occupation. In Lenski's Detroit survey, Catholics tended to favour working for large industrial corporations; Jews were inclined to professional careers; and Protestants were more entrepreneurial.

There is only a flimsy dividing line between beliefs about, and attitudes towards, economic issues and politics. In Britain, compared with many other societies, there is a tendency for religion and politics to be regarded as alternative forms of involvement. (Britain does not, of course, have anything like the religiously based political party system of some continental European societies.) Perhaps the most clear-cut feature of both the American and the British situations is the high percentage of those declaring themselves to have *no* religion who vote Democrat or Labour. In Britain, religious 'nones' are about three times more likely to vote Labour than Conservative.

There is some traceable flow from religious belief to political belief. Protestants tend to favour free-enterprise political ideologies and lack of state controls; the converse is true of Catholics. But one must set this against cross-cultural findings which suggest what Charles Y. Glock and Rodney Stark, in their *Religion and Society in Tension*, call 'the mutually corrosive' relationship between left-wing radicalism and religious commitment.

Much less is known about the relationships between religion and sexual behaviour. What information we do have relates very much to the social dimensions of religion. Studies undertaken in the 1950s along these lines, in Britain and America, showed less sexual activity among the highly religious. In terms of the average number of orgasms per week, and the amount of pre-marital sexual intercourse, particularly religious people were between a third and half as active sexually as the relatively non-religious. And this was true, with only minor differences, for all the major religious groups. Masturbation bore the same kind of relationship. The only sexual activity which appears to vary between major religious groups is homosexual intercourse. Jews have a low rate of *declared* (an important proviso) homosexuality, and Roman Catholics a high rate – notably those who say they are nominal or non-practising Catholics.

Racial prejudice provides an enlightening example of the problem of interpreting the influence on an individual of his religiosity. The difficulty here is not the lack of evidence but rather its conflicting nature. Michael Argyle's tentative summary, published in 1958, still appears to hold much truth. The highly religious – as indicated at that time in primarily social terms – tend to be less racially prejudiced than people who say they are only nominal adherents. But religious individuals in general are more prejudiced than the non-religious. Roman Catholics tend to be the most racially prejudiced; Jews and members of the smaller Christian sects the least prejudiced. The race-prejudice exception to the general conservatism of many sects is, in large part, due to salvational missioning – in other words, 'get members at all costs'.

There is an extensive variation within American Protestantism in respect of race prejudice, according to Stark and Glock's *American Piety*. The doctrinally heterodox are the least racially prejudiced (for example, Congregationalists). This contrasts with an orthodoxy/prejudice association among Southern Baptists and, to a lesser extent, among Missouri Lutherans. However, Lenski, in his Detroit study, found that there was no clearly discernible association between liberalism (a problematic concept, anyway) and doctrinal heterodoxy – except on freedom of speech.

One can only conclude that an important debate has been opened up. Recently, the problem has been further complicated by Milton Rokeach's study of Americans' religious values in relation to what he calls 'social compassion'. Rokeach found a much clearer association between religion (notably in terms of church attendance) and racial intolerance than previous survey research showed.

The fact that, both analytically and in the 'real world', there is so much variation in interpretation should be seen in conjunction with the general malleability of phenomena which are considered to be religious or closely related to religion. In recent years, this has been particularly true of Roman Catholicism. Some changes within the confines of Catholicism have been so recent that they constrain us to look very sceptically at studies, undertaken, say, in the 1950s which showed sharp differences between Catholics and Protestants. This is most obviously true of family life and sexual behaviour. The marked increase in the number of Roman Catholic women in Britain seeking and obtaining abortions is a major example. In this general sphere, it is also important that, in several European societies, Catholic/Protestant differences in family size have been nearly eliminated. Other changes within Catholicism, such as pentecostalist tendencies in some areas of America, mean that it is increasingly hard to predict an individual's other dispositions and attitudes on the basis of his religion.

Fortunately, there are signs that, precisely because the contemporary nature of 'the religious situation' is so puzzling, more and more social scientists are immersing themselves in the puzzles. 'Religion' is an exceedingly amorphous and 'fuzzy' variable; and the pay-offs for the efforts which have been put into making it more susceptible to manipulation have only just begun to come in. A major question remains. Will the development of more sophisticated methods of analysis keep pace with the complexities of religious change during the next few decades? For various reasons, the sociological study of religion has lagged behind other sections of the social sciences in terms of its methodological rigour. One of the critical factors — but, it should be stressed, only one among others — is that religious phenomena are more intractable analytically than most socio-cultural phenomena. It may well be that the recent concern — notably in America — with systematization and quantification in the study of religion will divert too much attention from such crucial problems as the apparent increase in subscription to superstitious beliefs, astrology, cultic belief systems, and so on. It is only those who regard themselves as sociologists of religion who are likely to devote intellectual energy to the study of such phenomena — at least in the community of social scientists.

Thus, what we may be gaining in terms of precise knowledge about the relationship between religion in its 'official' and institutional forms may be offset by an expansion of areas of substantive ignorance. In any case, much of what has been reported here in terms of fairly well established generalisations is based on survey methods of research, involving the use of sample surveys and closed-ended question schedules. The latter have become increasingly suspect as a mode of genuinely sociological analysis during the past few years. Many sociologists now favour one or another form of in-depth interview or, in some cases, experimental situations which try to overcome the artificiality of the closed-ended interview. These kinds of exploration are not easily susceptible to exact manipulation, and subsequent generalization, across different kinds of population. And yet in-depth probing of 'the religion of everyday life' might well cast some very significant light on the inconsistencies which are thrown up by more conventional methods treating religion as a 'face-sheet variable'. We have tended to operate in terms of very gross categories of social and cultural aspects of religiosity. The present malleability of religious phenomena suggests that we will not be able to persist with these for much longer.

The questions themselves vary. Gallup asks: 'If there were a general election tomorrow, which party would you support?' National Opinion Polls puts it slightly differently: 'How would you vote if there were a general election tomorrow?' The Butler/Stokes surveys, in addition to a standard voting-intention question, also ask: 'Generally speaking, do you usually think of yourself as Conservative, Labour or Liberal?'

But, whatever the wording, the aim of all of the questions is clear: to identify the respondent's party affiliation. Just as the question, 'What are his politics?' almost always means 'Which party does he support?', so party is one of the key variables in all political research – even when the researcher's main concern is with other things, like attitude formation or political participation.

'Party affiliation' is, however, a tricky concept to work with – much trickier than (say) age or sex. There are two reasons for this. One is that the phrase can mean quite different things. At one extreme, it can imply actual party membership, in the sense of someone joining a party and paying dues; at the other, it can refer to no more than someone's intention to vote for a particular party at a particular election. In between, it can refer either to an individual's voting record over the years (i.e. to his actual behaviour), or to his general predisposition, if he has one, to vote more often than not for one party rather than another (i.e. to his state of mind).

The other reason for party affiliation's being a tricky concept to work with is that a person's party affiliation, however defined, may not be stable. Basic psychological predispositions, once formed, tend to change only slowly over time; but changes in voting, in particular, are much more frequent than used to be thought. The idea still persists that the overwhelming majority of the British electorate is firmly attached to one party or the other, and that elections are decided by a relatively few 'floating' voters in the middle. In fact, we now know that even at two elections as close together as those of 1964 and 1966 only about 70 per cent of the electorate behaved consistently – i.e. voted for the same party at both elections or else stayed home. The remainder – nearly one third of the total – either changed parties or switched between voting and non-voting.

Because the concept is tricky in these ways, most of the generalizations contained in this chapter are only rough approximations to the truth. Nonetheless, mainly thanks to Butler and Stokes's *Political Change in Britain*, we can say far more about mass partisanship today than we could 20 years ago, and also say it with much greater confidence. We have to rely heavily on Butler/Stokes: not only is it the most recent study of Britain (most of the others date from the 1950s) but it is the only one based on repeated interviews with a large sample of electors covering the whole country.

If we know someone's party affiliation, what else do we know about him? Alternatively, if we know various other things about a person, what can we infer about his party leanings? The usual answers, as we shall see, are not always the right ones.

Most voters have acquired some sort of party affiliation by the time they are about 30 or 35; the young are much more changeable politically than the middle-aged and old. But where do the young acquire their partisan loyalties from? The obvious answer is 'from their parents'. And the obvious answer is partly true, but only partly. As Butler and Stokes put it, 'Partisanship over the individual's lifetime has some of the quality of a photographic reproduction that deteriorates with time: it is a fairly sharp copy of the parents' original at the beginning of political awareness, but over the years it becomes somewhat blurred, although remaining easily recognizable.'

What causes the blurring? If the family is thought of as one contender for the child's political allegiance, it would seem that it can have two main rivals. One is social class, where the party the parents support is not the party dominant in their class (i.e. where the parents are middle-class socialists or working-class Tories). The other is the political circumstances of the era in which the child grew up, where these run counter to the allegiance of the parents.

Butler and Stokes found that, whereas 85 per cent of children whose parents supported the dominant party in their class supported the same party themselves, only 58 per cent of the children whose parents supported the opposite party remained true to their parents' political faith; the other 42 per cent had been drawn away. Children were also likely to differ from their parents if, for example, their parents were Conservative at a time of great Labour strength like the years after 1945.

This raises, of course, the relationship between partisanship and age. The young at the moment are disproportionately Labour, the old disproportionately Conservative, with the middle aged tending to fall somewhere in between. The findings in table 1, which are typical of the last decade, are drawn from NOP's 1970 post-election survey:

Table 1 *Voting by age, 1970*

	18–24	25–34	35–44	45–54	55–64	65+
Conservative	42·3	41·0	46·1	43·3	47·5	56·2
Labour	47·2	45·8	40·6	49·1	43·7	37·1

But, as Philip Abrams points out in *Age and generation*, although these facts are clear, the explanation for them is less so. The popularly held view is that people, as they grow older, become more Conservative – with a capital 'C'. And this view is rather compelling: the old are apt to be set in their ways, and everyone can think of a friend or uncle who was radical in his youth (or claims he was), but who now votes Tory. But a much better explanation is one in terms of 'political generations'.

On this view, the preponderance of Conservatives among the over-65s is the result, not primarily of their being old as such, but of their having matured politically at a time when the Conservatives were the dominant party, and when Labour was only beginning to emerge as a political force. The old, in other words, may always be conservative, in the sense of being set in their ways politically; but they will not indefinitely be Conservative. The greater political constancy of old people emerges clearly from table 2, taken from Butler/Stokes. The dates in the top row are the dates at which respondents were first able to vote:

Table 2 *Voting constancy and age*

	Pre-1918	Inter-war	Post-1945	Post-1951
% supporting same party in 1959 and 1964	86	81	79	58

The photographic reproduction, showing how far children's voting resembles their parents, will naturally be especially blurred if the original photo itself was not very clear. Children are particularly prone to differ from their parents politically if they do not know which party their parents supported, or if their parents were divided. Under these circumstances – less common in Britain than in France or America – children are usually drawn towards the party of their class.

The problem of causation is as perplexing in political research as in any other social science. We know, for instance, that husbands and wives vote alike more often than not. The common belief is that this is because husbands influence their wives. But it could be – and undoubtedly sometimes is – because wives influence their husbands. It could also be – in fact, it probably usually is – because both husbands and wives are subject to the same social forces, of class, neighbourhood and prior conditioning.

With regard to the relationship between partisanship and sex, the problem of causation is particularly perplexing. Women are much more Conservative than men. Indeed, if only men had had the vote, Labour would have won every election since the war; only in 1966 did more women vote Labour than Conservative. The difference between the sexes is not enormous but it is considerable, as one can see from the figures in table 3 (the 1959 data is taken from Gallup, the rest from NOP):

Table 3 *Voting by sex*

General election	1959	1964	1966	1970
% difference between Conservative advantage among women and Conservative advantage among men	12	13	14	14

Oddly enough, almost no effort has gone into trying to explain this phenomenon. We know that the old are disproportionately Conservative, and also that there are more old women than old men; but this can account for only a fraction of the difference – and beyond this all is supposition and hypothesis. For example, Anglicans tend, as we shall see in a moment, to be Conservative, especially those who go to church; moreover, more women than men are Anglicans and more women than men are regular church attenders. Yet, even within the category of regular church attenders, the women are fractionally more Tory-inclined than the men. Why should this be so? No one knows. Nor is anyone sure – to take another example – why spinsters seem to be more Conservative than bachelors.

Another causal puzzle concerns the connection between trade union membership and voting. With one minor exception, every survey ever conducted in Britain has shown that workers who belong to trade unions vote Labour more often than workers who do not. And the conclusion has almost invariably been drawn; there is something about being a union member which conduces towards Labour allegiance in politics. It was left to Butler and Stokes to explore the contrary hypothesis: not that union membership inclines workers towards Labour, but that it is workers who are already Labour-inclined who are readiest to join unions. They concentrated their attention on workers who had joined their union voluntarily – or had refused to join. The gist of their findings, supporting their views, is set out in table 4:

Table 4 *Trade unionism and Labour voting*

Voluntary trade-union members:	Labour%, 1964
1. 'Some' workmates are members	87
2. 'Most' workmates are members	63
3. 'All' workmates are members	54
asked to join and have refused	40

Willingness (or not) to vote Labour, and willingness (or not) to join unions, depends partially on where an individual lives. Different parts of the country have had strikingly different histories: industry came to them in different forms and at different times; so did unemployment. It would be surprising if, in the different regions, the past had not left a firm imprint on the present. Likewise, in towns and cities, even along a particular street, if one party is dominant locally, residents are more likely to conform to the local political culture. What they sense 'in the air' will be reinforced by workplace and neighbourhood face-to-face contacts.

The facts about place and partisanship, indeed, give the lie to the belief, still widely held, that the British landscape is uniform politically – and that geography does not matter. Blondel and Butler/Stokes have both shown that, within each social class, support for the political parties varies widely from region to region. For example, a manual worker is twice as likely to vote Conservative in the south west as in Wales. Table 5, adapted from Butler/Stokes, conveys some idea of the scale of within-class regional differences:

Table 5 *Voting intention by region and class 1963–66*

	London/SE	SW	E Midlands	NE	Wales
Con. AB	74·1	77·4	83·2	72·7	58·0
Lab.	13·0	9·9	8·9	18·6	30·8
Con. C2	33·6	38·2	33·5	26·5	15·2
Lab.	56·0	46·9	59·0	69·2	79·9

The same researchers have also shown that, even within particular regions, the influence of town and neighbourhood can be powerful. Bealey and his colleagues found in Newcastle-under-Lyme that workers living in predominantly middle class districts were significantly more likely to vote Tory than their mates in other parts of town; this was probably partly the result of Toryish workers seeking to live in Toryish neighbourhoods, but not wholly. Such self-selection cannot even begin to account for one of the most spectacular Butler/Stokes findings. They compared, within each social class, residents of mining communities and residents of seaside resorts. Someone who thought of himself as middle class, they discovered, was five times more likely to vote Labour if he lived in a mining community than if he lived in a resort. Likewise, workers living in resorts were nearly six times more likely than workers in mining communities to vote Conservative.

With regard to religion, too, the past is still visible in the present. The Tory party is no longer the Church of England in politics; but the Church of England is still, to a remarkable degree, the Tory party at prayer. Milne and Mackenzie found in 1955, and every survey has agreed since, that, even today, an Anglican is much more likely to be a Conservative than (say) a Roman Catholic or a Methodist. And an Anglican who attends church regularly is much more likely to be a Conservative than one who does not; Butler and Stokes found in 1963 that, among those who went to church once a year or less, 38 per cent were Conservatives; whilst among those who went at least once a week, no less than 72 per cent were Tories.

The relationship between religion and politics is, of course, more complicated than this implies: in particular, both religion and politics are to a high degree a function of social class, the middle classes being disproportionately both Tories and Anglicans and church-goers. But, even within the two classes, regular church attendance is powerfully associated with political Conservatism. Church-going workers and their wives are much more likely to identify with the Tories than their Roman Catholic, Non-conformist or secular mates; church-goers are even more likely to be Conservative than others in the middle classes.

Nevertheless, the ties between religion and politics are becoming frayed. They are largely a legacy of the past and, outside Northern Ireland, are not being reinforced by current developments. In 1963, among those who had first been eligible to vote before 1918, working-class Anglicans were far more likely to be Conservative than middle-class Anglicans were to be Liberal or Labour, whilst among Nonconformists the reverse was true. By contrast, among those eligible to vote in 1951 or after, the class differences within each denomination show signs of diminishing to the vanishing point. The working class Anglican Tory will fairly soon, it seems, turn into a figure of the past.

It should already be evident that social class is not the only determinant of party allegiance. Someone may be a manual worker and trade-union member, yet not vote Labour because of his family background, religion or residence – or possibly because, as John Goldthorpe has shown us in *The Affluent Worker*, a lot of the people he associates with are in white-collar occupations. Likewise, there are all sorts of reasons why not everyone in the solid middle classes is a Tory. Even if none of this were true, moreover, class could still not be the sole determinant of voting, since changes in voting are far more rapid and frequent than changes in individuals' class location.

Nonetheless, class and party allegiance are closely linked in Britain. Indeed the links between class and party are closer than between party and any other single nonpolitical factor. As the class-and-region table shows, even in Wales well over half of those in the top social strata are Tory supporters; even in the south west nearly half of the skilled manual workers back Labour. The forging of these links occurred early in this century, in the circumstances that gave rise to Labour and eventually destroyed the Liberals.

The aspect of the class/party link that has most tantalized researchers is the heavy weight of Conservative voting amongst manual workers. For one thing, the working classes are more numerous than the middle classes, so that, even if everyone in both classes had an equal propensity to defect to the opposite party, working class Tories would still, in absolute numbers, overbalance middle class Labour supporters. For another, it seemed to be the case that the propensity to defect was not in fact equal in the two classes, and that, even proportionately, 'wrong-party' voting was much more common amongst the workers. Two separate studies, by Nordlinger, and McKenzie and Silver, both conceived before Labour's victory in 1964, were devoted to exploring this phenomenon.

And wrong-party voting remains of interest; Labour supporters in the middle classes, in particular, have never been studied seriously. But two factors have caused working-class Conservatism no longer seem of unique importance. The first is the discovery that manual workers, as they become more materially affluent, do not, at least not in large numbers, become Tory-inclined. Goldthorpe and his colleagues found that the prosperous workers of Luton showed no long-term tendency to lean more towards the Conservatives as their incomes increased. In 1963–4 Butler and Stokes found – somewhat to their own surprise – that voters who moved into better housing at this time were more, not less, likely to favour Labour, despite the overall national swing back to the Conservatives that took place before the 1964 election.

The second factor depriving working class Conservatism of some of its old fascination is the discovery that it is on the decline. As the Labour Party comes of age electorally, the proportion of workers with a strong disposition to vote Tory is diminishing – to the point where, proportionately, they are hardly more numerous than middle-class Labour incliners. Table 6 tells the story.

But party allegiance is not solely a function of social position, whether defined in class terms or in any other way; in the end it is a function of opinion. A man may be aged thirty-two, be a staunch Methodist, live in a mining

Table 6 *Cross-class voting*

voters first eligible to vote				
	Pre-1918	Inter-war	1945	Post-1951
Difference between % of working class supporting Con. and % of middle class supporting Lab.	33	16	2	6

community in the north east, have parents both of whom vote Labour, he himself a pit worker and a strong trade unionist, and have no friends or contacts in the middle classes; but if – despite all this – he still believes that Edward Heath is a saint, Harold Wilson a sinner, and that the Tories will be more successful than Labour in improving the economic situation of himself and his family, it is quite probable that he will vote Conservative.

There is, however, no very neat fit between the opinions of the political parties, as manifested in speeches and party programmes, and the opinions of those who elect them. Blondel showed for the years 1959–61 that differences between the two parties on social and economic issues are broadly mirrored amongst their supporters in the electorate, but that their differences on foreign and 'conscience' issues were not.

More recently, Butler and Stokes have produced evidence of similar slippages, and have also shown that on important current issues many voters do not have any developed opinions at all. For example, a sample of voters were asked in the summer of 1963, and again in the autumn of 1964, whether they favoured the nationalization of a lot more industries, a few more, or no more; or whether they would like to see some industries denationalized. Even though the nationalization issue had been politically salient for a quarter-century, only 39 per cent of the total sample gave the same reply at both interviews. It is clear from other evidence that the unstable majority consisted, not of people who had genuinely changed their minds, but mainly of those who, lacking true opinions, were responding to the questionnaire more or less at random.

Furthermore, just as one cannot infer an individual's opinions on specific current issues from his party affiliation, so one cannot infer that he shares his party's ideology, at least not in any full-blown sense. Butler and Stokes found in Britain, as their colleagues had already discovered in America, that although there is a certain consistency in the attitudes of many voters, few can be described in any sense as bearers of ideology. Not only are the great majority of electors innocent of anything that could be called an ideological vocabulary (60 per cent have no idea what the terms 'right' and 'left' connote); more important, their opinions on issues form no intellectually coherent pattern, with only modest correlations amongst opinions on such doctrinally salient matters as nationalization and trade union and business power.

The opinions that determine party allegiance are not those on issues determined by parties or ideologists. They are those on issues – and values and images – that the electors themselves deem important. These vary from time to time. In the recent past, they have included the parties' perceived relationship to the social classes, especially the working class; the images of the parties and their leaders; and the governing party's perceived success, or lack of it, in preventing unemployment and ensuring stable prices. An individual's opinions on these questions are powerfully influenced by his place in society; but they are not finally determined by it. Man, it seems, is a political as well as a social animal.

Some Conclusions
R. E. Pahl

The various chapters in this book have attempted to judge how much difference income, education, marital status, and so forth, make for given individuals. It is significant that there are few variable imperialists who want to insist that their own variable accounts for more than somebody else's. Indeed, it is perhaps significant that most of the contributors have been more concerned about what they can *not* explain. They emphasize that they are at best referring to probabilities and not precise predictions, and that specific variables by themselves are far less important than the combination of several variables even as predictors of probabilities. It is also significant that there is no separate piece on 'class' or on 'status'. But more of that later.

Sociology is sometimes disliked, or perhaps feared, because it appears to be so insulting to people: it implies that one or two variables, like 'occupation' or 'education', determine a large proportion of people's lives. Such a sociology would seem to make people two-dimensional and flat, and it is perhaps this that causes most irritation or resentment. Critics of the subject could enjoy themselves with this book: a good cross-section of British sociologists have addressed themselves to what many would see as the key variables, and have in general concluded that each does not contribute as much as one might think. Perhaps this series is a clever ploy by Paul Barker, as the editor of *New Society*, to expose sociology's credibility gap. Unwittingly, each contributor to the series may have added to the overall conclusion that the Emperor has no clothes.

Yet, of course, to acknowledge that one does not know *everything* is not the same as saying one knows *nothing*.

Let us, in the traditional sociological fashion, postulate some ideal-typical views of *A Sociological Portrait*.

First, the number-crunching empiricist is likely to say that nowadays, with computers and other hardware, the question, 'What difference does it make', involves 'multi-variate analysis'. In this, instead of fitting variables together like a jigsaw puzzle, the sociologist superimposes them on one another like a sieve map, and uses *bundles* of variables or components in his analysis. Also, he puts the variables in a context or chooses them in relation to specific hypotheses. Thus, instead of just asking general questions about what difference religion or income makes, he will be more likely to pose the issue in connection with, say, Northern Ireland (i.e. 'What difference does religion make in Ulster?') or the inner city (i.e. 'What difference does income make in Islington?'). In other words, our typical empiricist might argue that the series' approach might be, in broad terms, correct, but that it was set up in too simple a way.

The second ideal-type I would call the traditional theoretician. Such a sociologist looks to Marx, Weber and Durkheim as his mentors and is concerned with 'important sociological questions', like social order and social change. He might dismiss the empiricist as a market research specialist, and claim that to ask what difference a social variable makes in *individual* behaviour, is to turn sociology on its head: no self-respecting sociologist should attempt to answer it. Society is not to be understood in terms of contemporary social statistics alone, but in terms of broad historical trends and economic power relationships.

A very good example of this 'ideal-type' in action appeared in *Sociology* in 1970, when G. K. Ingham criticized

W. G. Runciman for emphasising individual attributes when discussing stratification. Runciman, as author of *Relative Deprivation and Social Justice*, wrote an essay on 'Class, status and power?' in which he maintained that each of these three dimensions of a stratification order were conceptually distinct and that, in certain circumstances, individuals could be ranked so that they appear at different places on each dimension. (He also went on to say that, 'On the whole, a man's occupation is a fairly reliable index of his relative position in all three dimensions.') Ingham objected to this emphasis on an individual's attributes which can be measured and claimed that: 'The founders of the classic sociological tradition of stratification analysis – Marx and Weber – were not merely concerned with the attributional aspects of class and even less with wealth and income as indicators of "class situation"'. Marx, in fact, specifically rejected such an oversimple view of class in his usual robust way: "Vulgar common sense turns class differences into differences in the size of one's purse and class conflict into a quarrel between handicrafts".'

In line with this, the traditional theoretician would argue that diverting attention to individuals reflects a certain ideology. It distracts from 'true sociological concerns, such as the nature and stability of élites, or the 'proletarianization' of certain categories of white collar workers. Class is not simply an association of variables, but is a dynamic element in social change.

Finally, there is a flourishing and rapidly expanding ideal-type who would question the basic validity of all the data which purport to connect a specific variable with specific behaviour. Those adopting this stance would claim that there never can be a direct relationship between so-called 'objective' characteristics and social action. The crucial factor is the *meaning* put on the attribute or variable by the actor concerned. When someone claims, for example, that 'You're as young as you feel,' this may be a much more valid comment than any attempt to allocate typical behaviour to specific age categories.

The meaning of being married, the meaning of religious adherence, the meaning of specific localities, the meaning of specific family relationships, all vary enormously. These meanings are themselves related to other variables: age, occupation, income, religion, politics, and so forth, all take on different meanings, depending on our socialization within the family. Certainly, there is a sense in which we can never leave our natal family, since crucial experiences are internalized and carried with us throughout our life and therefore affect our interpretations of all experience.

Those who adopt this position may call themselves 'symbolic interactionists' or 'ethnomethodologists', which may not do much to endear them to the sceptical viewer of the Emperor's nakedness. However, they do, in fact, have much in common with him. (And they do also, of course, have much in common with many parts of this book.)

When the individual claims that he does not believe that he is a puppet responding to a cluster of role expectations, and following a life style determined by occupation, education and income characteristics, the symbolic interactionist listens to him with respect. When he responds in a confused and ambiguous fashion to a set of questions, he is not classified as a bad respondent or assigned to the 'Don't Know' category: rather, the issue of communication and interpretation is itself taken as problematic. The taken-for-granted assumptions of sociologists are themselves subject for study. Social life returns, in all its complexity, ambiguity, precariousness and confusion. It could be argued that this is the final, healthy upshot of *A Sociological Portrait*.

I have mentioned three possible reactions – not exhaustive, and certainly over-simplified – which, for different reasons, reject the single-variable approach. However, a counter-critic might well turn the attack: 'Is it then the case that you can say *nothing* about the influence of age, sex, income, marital status, politics and so forth on the individual? What have you been doing all these years, asking all these questions, if you haven't produced some conclusions?' Since these are by common consent 'sociological' variables, is it possible to attempt to disown them, in the ways at least two of my three ideal types imply?

I believe that there *is* a sociological value in *A Sociological Portrait*, and that the whole, is, to an extent, greater than the sum of its parts. If one considers the chapters on individual variables as a whole, one can draw certain general conclusions.

First, in this great advanced industrial society of ours, it is as well to remember that 'ascriptive' factors – those that you cannot choose – still dominate. Sex and family of origin emerge as of fundamental importance. Of course, the question arises, 'Important for what?'; and the answer is unhappily vague, such as 'position in the social structure' or 'life-chances'. In other words, for example, in determining basic life-chances, family influences education more than education influences family.

Secondly, the book shows that the interconnections between variables are often very much more important than a single variable. Thus, old age combined with low income, or locality combined with religious affiliation, provide potent indicators of individual behaviour and way of life.

Thirdly, it is good to have it made clear that objective factors may tell one something, but that they cannot finally be divorced from their subjective context. Paradoxically, it seems to me that, with this *Portrait*, sociology as a humanistic perspective gains over the positivist fundamentalism which views sociology as a social science. We can, with a clear conscience, bring people back in!

Fourthly, however, this must not be seen as a Great Leap Backwards. Even if social life is not *determined* by key variables, it certainly can be very severely *constrained* by them. Very few retired manual workers can holiday in Greece, and few large property owners are likely to be members of the Communist Party. We are still able to make fairly safe correlations at the extremes. The important thing is not to confuse correlations with explanations. And we must recall that many individuals are not at the extreme, but are 'men in the middle'.

But should there not have been a chapter specifically on 'class'? The answer depends again on the sociological perspective one adopts.

For our first type of sociologist – the up-to-date empiricist – a chapter on class would be so potent that many of the other chapters would not be necessary. If the class construct of socio-economic variables were appropriately weighted, then *by definition* it would account for the most variance, since its very construction would be based on its capacity to account for this variation. The construct would not 'explain' anything: it would simply be the most useful statistical term to cover a scale of broadly defined life-chances.

The theoretically-oriented sociologist in the classical tradition would also set much store by a chapter on class. But he would choose empirical information in a highly selective way, to exemplify his own interpretation of the relationship between the emergent classes and either the productive substructure or a system of markets. A chapter on class would be concerned with a discussion of significance, more than of empirical fact. Few sociologists heavily influenced by Marx would seriously discuss the details of an individual's life-style. The problem of the future of capitalism is a long way from the question of what difference marital status or location makes.

The interactionist, however, might feel differently. What, after all, is the meaning of stratification? Since there is widespread acceptance of the fact that we live in a class society, but widespread confusion about the implication of this, it might be more appropriate to consider the subjective impact of the objective factual order on an individual. Since most people are in a state of almost total misinformation about the *pattern* of inequality, then in that sense the facts do not exist and there would be little of substance in the chapter.

My view is that a chapter headed, 'What difference does class make?' could be seen as a call to revolution. In a society where the pattern of objective inequality is persistent, deep-rooted and, if anything, becoming increasingly unequal, the clear presentation of such facts might be expected to have clear political implications. Class inequality is a cumulative fact. It must encompass the distribution of power and resources, workplace inequality, educational opportunity, and access to public resources, facilities and information, and so on. But where men do not *define* the society as unequal, the consequences are that in a sense it 'really' is not unequal. People live by their own definitions of reality and not by sociologists' definitions, however 'true' these may be.

Sometimes the two can converge. I remember once trying to teach an adult class in a New Town about social class in Britain, and having no success at all. Despite considerable workplace inequality and so forth, all my students could see was their common ability to fill their homes with consumer goods. As it happened, my point was made for me very dramatically before the next week's session. The government decided it had quite enough guided missiles stored away for the time being, and so cut its contracts.

The resulting redundancy hit members of my group. and I had no difficulty in discussing class. The transparency of the situation led to a flicker of new awareness. But it didn't last long.

Class is a way of conceptualizing inequality. Thus, it is no less 'real' today than at any other time in this century, since the basic occupational structure and distribution of pay has remained stable throughout the period. The labels, 'middle class' and 'working class', roughly correspond with the distinction between non-manual and manual workers. Admittedly, there is a wide range of styles and cultures within each of these broad categories; these styles and cultures are often termed 'status groups'. However, such internal differences are overshadowed by the extent of the differences in life-chances between those in the middle of each of the two major class categories. Sometimes sociologists may seem to imply that class is the *source* of objective inequalities, such as the pattern of educational opportunity. This is not so: class is a *product* of inequality. So it is not possible to consider class and status as 'variables' like age and sex, precisely because these are conceptual and not simply descriptive terms. Hence their necessary omission as specific subject-headings in this series.

In the 'real' world of interpersonal relationships, the trivial seems to gain precedence over the fundamental, if I may be forgiven some value-laden words. When two men meet in a train, they can 'place' each other by clothes, accent, reading matter, and various visible signs of position in society. Each can do this without knowing whether the other is kind, generous or amusing. There appears to be a common value system which ties certain superficial signs to the hierarchy of prestige, based on the division of labour, that provides certain coordinates, so that you can roughly equate bowler hat, rolled umbrella and *The Times* with one occupation level; and cap, thermos, sandwich tin and strong boots with another.

Since their experience of others at some distance from themselves in society will be extraordinarily limited, our two men in the train may be virtually incapable of any communication, even if they are in the same 'class' of carriage. Each may roughly stereotype the other, and try a few conversational gambits. It is possible that they may discover some common ground in, for example, locality of origin or experience in the armed services. But without such links, communication breaks down.

The point I am making is that *neither* party 'sees' the important differences in class situation which affects how the other lives. Sitting in that train, neither has in mind, for example, such differences in their work situation as holidays, pensions, redundancy arrangements, clocking in, canteens, and where to go for a wash – all of which cumulatively lead to considerable class differences. Each sees the other in somewhat 'superficial' terms. Or should one say 'symbolic'? For the rolled umbrella or the thermos flask are symbols of *some* difference, even if they do not reflect adequately the range and intensity of inequality. If these images of class status have more salience than the 'facts' sociologists document, then more sociologists should follow Frank Parkin, in his *Class Inequality and Political Order*, and investigate the symbolic structures and meaning system which mask objective inequality.

So perhaps it is salutory not to have a section on class and status, if only to make one pose these questions. There is, I think, a new humility in sociology. Perhaps this book will help indicate the change that is taking place within the subject, in putting back the humanity where this had sometimes been lost.

Notes on Further Reading

These are notes supplied by the authors of the various chapters.

Place of publication of books is London, except where otherwise indicated.

Some books crop up more than once; but as this duplication seemed likely to be useful to anyone whose interest lay in a particular chapter, it has not been ironed out.

1 Income

The literature on income distribution is vast, and income cannot really be treated as separate from wealth for many purposes. A starting point, with references to much of the earlier literature, would be R. M. Titmuss, *Income Distribution and Social Change* (Allen & Unwin, 1962). E. Gittus, 'Income', in M. Stacey (ed.), *Comparability in Social Research* (Heinemann Educational, 1969) is a useful introduction to the problems of data collection and Alan F. Sillitoe, *Britain in Figures* (Penguin, 1971) contains useful summary data.

I have depended heavily on the latest report in the invaluable series, *Family Expenditure Survey, Report for 1970* (HMSO, 1971). H. Lydall, *The Structure of Earnings* (Oxford University Press, 1968) is a very technical account. On the ownership of property and income derived from it, see J. E. Meade, *Efficiency, Equality and the Ownership of Property* (Allen & Unwin, 1964). There is also an extensive review of the literature to be found in R. Miliband, *The State in Capitalist Society* (Weidenfeld & Nicholson, 1969), though the book is of course concerned with a much wider theme.

Much the same problem of choice confronts us in the field of poverty but P. Townsend (ed.), *The Concept of Poverty* (Heinemann, 1970), and K. Coates and R. Silburn, *Poverty: the forgotten Englishmen* (Penguin, 1970) are both excellent and contain many useful references for further reading. D. Bull (ed.), *Family Poverty* (Duckworth, 1971) is focused on a particular aspect of the problem but contains much more of general interest, as does A. B. Atkinson, *Poverty in Britain and the Reform of Social Security* (Cambridge University Press, 1970) which is, however, more technical. M. Harrington, *The Other America* (Penguin, 1963), was at least partly responsible for the 'rediscovery of poverty' and is still worth reading.

The general literature on social class does not concern us directly but J. H. Goldthorpe, D. Lockwood, F. Bechhofer and J. Platt, *The Affluent Worker in the Class Structure* (Cambridge University Press, 1969) is concerned partly with the question of income and class. Incidental material on consumption, income and saving patterns, particularly in the working class, can be found in many monographs but a useful summary source with many references is Josephine Klein, *Samples from English Cultures*, vol 1 (Routledge & Kegan Paul, 1965). Colin Bell, *Middle Class Families* (Routledge & Kegan Paul, 1968) is one of the few relevant studies of the middle class.
Frank Bechhofer

2 Occupation

There are chapters in several recently published British books which deal with aspects of the sociology of occupations – for example, chapter 4, 'Work', in E. Butterworth and D. Weir (eds.), *The Sociology of Modern Britain* (Fontana, 1970); chapter 5, 'Work, industry and organizations', in P. Worsley *et al*, *Introducing Sociology* (Penguin, 1970); and some chapters in A. Fox, *A Sociology of Work in Industry* (New York: Collier-Macmillan, 1971). But for book-length treatment of the subject one has to turn to the Americans: T. Caplow, *The Sociology of Work* (New York: McGraw-Hill, 1964) is a good general introduction to the whole field, and M. L. Taylor, *Occupational Sociology* (New York: Oxford University Press, 1968), is a broad overview dealing with most aspects from occupational structures to meanings of work.

P. L. Berger (ed.), *The Human Shape of Work* (New York: Macmillan, 1964) is a collection of articles dealing with attitudes of various occupational groups, while F. Herzberg, *Work and the Nature of Man* (Staples Press, 1968) tackles the same subject with a different (motivation-hygiene) theory. S. Nosow's chapter, 'Social correlates of occupational membership', in S. Nosow and W. H. Form (eds.), *Man, Work, and Society* (New York: Basic Books, 1962) is a useful review of the literature. For a fascinating series of autobiographical case-studies of what work means to people in various occupations, see R. Fraser (ed.), *Work: Twenty Personal Accounts* (Penguin, vol. 1, 196j; vol. 2, 1969). The complex relationship between occupational and leisure life is dealt with in S. R. Parker, *The Future of Work and Leisure* (Paladin, 1972).

S. R. Parker

3 Sex Differences

Most standard books on individual differences contain chapters on the way in which the sexes differ. Two good examples of books of this sort are A. Anastasi, *Differential Psychology: individual and group differences in behaviour* (New York: Macmillan, third edition, 1958), and L. E. Tyler, *The Psychology of Human Differences* (New York: Appleton-Century-Crofts, 1965). From the point of view of the student, however, a better starting point might be E. E. Maccoby's *The Development of Sex Differences*

(Tavistock, 1967). In this book, chapters by different authors are devoted to different theories on how sex differences arise, and there is at the end a very comprehensive, annotated bibliography of the subject.

Recently, two books have been published on the psychology of women by J. A. Sherman (*On the Psychology of Women;* Springfield, Illinois, Charles C. Thomas, 1971) and by J. M. Bardwick (*Psychology of Women;* Harper & Row, 1971). These books also contain reviews of the evidence on how the sexes differ. Finally, there is *Sex, Gender and Society* by Ann Oakley (Temple Smith, in association with *New Society*, 1972). This contains a great deal of factual information which is linked to a strong defence of the view that sex differences are overwhelmingly due to cultural influences.

Derek Wright

4 Family Background

Where feasible, I have named my sources in the text; and where these are not traceable through the contents or the bibliographies of the works listed below, a good library and a considerate librarian should help.

Much of the factual material on Britain is summarized in Josephine Klein, *Samples from English Cultures*, vol 2 (Routledge & Kegan Paul, 1965). Two of the most productive research projects have reported their findings in several volumes: J. and E. Newson, *Infant Care in an Urban Community* and *Four Years Old in an Urban Community* (Allen & Unwin, 1963 and 1968), and J. W. B. Douglas *et al*, *The Home and the School* (MacGibbon and Kee, 1964) and *All our Future* (Davies, 1968). Two other interesting studies are Hannah Gavron, *The Captive Wife* (Penguin, 1968) and Hilary Land, *Large Families in London* (Bell, 1968).

There is much in Liam Hudson, *The Ecology of Human*

Intelligence (Penguin, 1970), including the paper by Moss and Kagan, and in a forthcoming collection of essays on the earlier years, M. P. M. Richards, *The Integration of the Child into the Social World* (Cambridge University Press, 1973), including the paper by Ainsworth and Bell. This may be supplemented by a good general text, such as R. Brown, *Social Psychology* (Collier Macmillan, 1965). The more specifically sociological literature on what is usually called 'socialization' is generally poor, and not worth consulting. It is characterized more by bland assertion from within an *a priori* scheme than by reasoned argument and critical evidence.

There are of course many articles, but four that seem to me to be of especial interest are: E. C. Devereux Jr (in R. Hill, R. Konig, *Families in East and West*, Paris and The Hague: Mouton, 1970); M. L. Kohn (*American Journal of Sociology* vol. 68, 1963); D. Oldham, B. Bytheway, G. Horobin (*Journal of Biosocial Science, Supplement 3*, 1971); and A. L. Stinchcombe (*Harvard Educational Review*, vol 39, 1969).

Lastly, it is definitely worth looking at the various descriptions by R. D. Laing of interactions within families and their effects, although it should be remembered that we have no idea how typical such patterns may be.
Geoffrey Hawthorn

5 Marital Status

The approach to marriage that underlies this article is derived from the classic writings of Durkheim – notably as worked out by Peter Berger and Hansfried Kellner in their article, ' Marriage and the construction of reality' which originally appeared in *Diogenes* in 1964 but has recently been reprinted in *School and Society: a Sociological Reader* (Routledge & Kegan Paul, 1971), edited by B. R.

Cosin, I. R. Dale, G. M. Esland and D. R. Swift. Influential descriptions of the social conditions of some marriages in America can be found in Robert O. Blood and Donald M. Wolfe, *Husbands and Wives* (Free Press, 1969) and Mirra Komarovsky, *Blue Collar Marriage* (New York: Random House, 1962). This country is less well served, but there is the seminal contribution of Elizabeth Bott in her *Family and Social Network* (Tavistock, 1957) and Josephine Klein summarized the descriptive material available up to the early 1960s in her *Samples from English Cultures* (Routledge & Kegan Paul, 1965).

Dennis Marsden's brilliant *Mothers Alone* (Allen Lane, 1969) and Peter Marris's *Widows and their families* (Routledge & Kegan Paul, 1968) begin the study of the unmarried in this country. William J. Goode's *After Divorce* (Glencoe: The Free Press, 1956) is a path-breaking study of divorced women in America. Two American texts are useful – Willard Waller and Reuben Hill's remarkable *The Family* (New York: Holt, Rinehart & Winston, 1938, revised edition 1951) and Ralph Turner's, *Family Interaction* (New York: Wiley, 1970). C. C. Harris's *The Family* (Allen & Unwin, 1969) is the best short sociological introduction on the topic. There is a valuable collection of papers in the reader edited by Michael Anderson, *The Family* (Penguin, 1970). R. S. Weiss speculates on 'Marriage and the family in the near future' in *The Family and its Future*, (edited by Katherine Elliot J. and A. Churchill. 1970).

The view of the family as a destructive social unit is represented by the work of R. D. Laing – for example, his *The Politics of the Family* (Tavistock, 1971) or more extremely by David Cooper's *The Death of the Family* (Tavistock, 1971). This has recently been visualized in Ken-Loach's film, *Family Life*.

Data about marriage and the family can be found in

Peter Willmott's 'Some social trends' (*Urban Studies*, vol 6, No. 3, 1969), issues of *Social Trends* (HMSO), and various census volumes. That some of these data do not always mean what they appear to mean, can be seen in two important recent papers by Robert Chester, 'The duration of marriage to divorce' (*British Journal of Sociology*, vol 22, No. 2, 1971) and 'Contemporary trends in the stability of English marriage' (*Journal of Biosocial Science*, No. 3, 1971).

Other data in my chapter comes from the various census volumes.

Colin Bell

6 Friends and Associates

This chapter owes much to the overall perspective developed in a book by McCall and Simmons – G. J. McCall and J. L. Simmons, *Identities and Interactions* (Glencoe: The Free Press, 1966) – particularly parts of chapter 4 ('persons strive to fulfil their own expectations of themselves, not social expectations', page 91) and chapter 8, 'The interactive career of the individual.'

The symbolic interactionist perspective is perhaps best approached through the writings of Herbert Blumer. His most important essays are reprinted in *Symbolic Interactionism: Perspective and Method* (Englewood Cliffs, New Jersey: Prentice Hall, 1969) and the first chapter is a clear and previously unpublished presentation of the methodological position. An approach to the study of reference groups from this perspective is provided by T. Shibutani's 'Reference groups and social control', in A. M. Rose (ed.), *Human Behaviour and Social Processes* (Routledge & Kegan Paul, 1962).

Perhaps the simplest way to view many of the most important issues in more traditional reference group theory is to dip into the selection edited by H. H. Hyman and E. Singer, *Readings in Reference Group Theory and Research* (New York: Collier-Macmillan, 1968). The introduction is most useful. The classical source for much of the later discussion is S. A. Stouffer's *The American Soldier: Adjustment during Army Life* (Princeton University Press. 1949). However, most readers will probably prefer to read W. G. Runciman's stimulating presentation in *Relative Deprivation and Social Justice* (Penguin edition, 1972).

The concept of social network is best approached through the work of social anthropologists who have developed the concept after extensive fieldwork. A good selection of this work is available in J. C. Mitchell (ed.), *Social Networks in Urban Situations* (Manchester University Press, 1969). Finally, for a strongly positivistic orientation to friendship see R. K. Merton 'Friendship as a social process: a substantive and methodological analysis', in *Freedom and Control in Modern Society*, edited by M. Berger, T. Abel and C. Page (Van Nostrand, 1954).
R. E. Pahl

7 Location

R. E. Pahl has edited a most useful collection of essays that includes discussion of whether and to what extent spatial social segregation does occur in cities (*Readings in Urban Sociology*; Oxford: Pergamon, 1968). His *Patterns of Urban Life* (Longmans, 1970) is also addressed to the same question. For a formal examination of the Chicago School concepts of concentric and sector structures of urban areas, and hence of models of urban social structure, D. W. G. Timm's *The Urban Mosaic: towards a theory of residential differentiation* (Cambridge University Press, 1971), is undoubtedly the best study. And B. T. Robson's *Urban Analysis: a study of city structure with special reference to*

Sunderland (Cambridge University Press, 1969) is to be commended for its careful use of multivariate analysis on data for one city.

As for the future, the most provocative writings are probably L. Wingo (ed.), *Cities and Space: the future of urban land* (Baltimore: Johns Hopkins Press, 1963), which includes an important essay by M. Webber; and Peter Hall's *London 2000* (Faber, first published in 1963).

At the regional scale, several books warrant attention, including C. A. Moser and W. Scott, *British Towns: a statistical study of their social and economic differences* (Edinburgh: Oliver & Boyd, 1961). The books by G. Taylor and N. Ayres *(Born and Bred Unequal;* Longman, 1969) and B. E. Coates and E. M. Rawstron *(Regional Variations in Britain;* Batsford, 1971) both provide a wealth of descriptive information about the contemporary spatial variations of both social and economic phenomena. The historical background to these differences is provided by C. H. Lee in *Regional Economic Growth in the United Kingdom Since the 1880s* (McGraw-Hill, 1971).

For a more analytical examination of regional differences, the best works are probably G. McCrone, *Regional Policy in Britain* (Allen & Unwin, 1969), and M. Chisholm and G. Manners (eds.) *Spatial Policy Problems of the British Economy* (Cambridge University Press, 1971). Finally, as an example of a specific social issue – the geographical variation in the number of children separated from their parents and 'in care' – the reader could well turn to J. Packman, *Child Care: needs and numbers* (Allen & Unwin, 1968).

Three important references in my chapter are: A. Giggs, 'Socially disorganised areas in Barry: a multivariable analysis', in H. Carter and W. K. D. Davies, (eds.) *Urban Essays: studies in the geography of Wales* (Longman, 1970); L. Wirth, 'Urbanism as a way of life' (*American Journal*

of Sociology, No. 44, 1938); and Emrys Jones and D. J. Sinclair, *Atlas of London* (Pergamon, 1971).
Michael Chisholm

8 Age and Generation

The study of age is intimately bound up with the study of the social organization and meaning of time. Two books which usefully open up the discussion of this relationship of age to time are W. E. Moore, *Man, Time and Society* (New York, Wiley, 1963), and S. De Grazia, *Of Time, Work and Leisure* (New York: Anchor Books, 1964).

The problems of life cycle and its critical phases are well treated in, for example, T. H. Bossard, *Parent and Child* (Philadelphia: University of Pennsylvania Press, 1953), who has an interesting analysis of the *rites de passage* associated with movement from one age grade to another; F. Musgrove, *Youth and the Social Order* (Routledge & Kegan Paul, 1964), who among other things treats the 'invention' of adolescence as a social institution; R. Kleemeier, *Ageing and Leisure* (New York: Oxford University Press, 1961), who assembles a rich body of empirical data on the situation, experience and activities of the old; and especially in S. N. Eisenstadt, *From Generation to Generation* (Routledge & Kegan Paul, 1956). Eisenstadt's book is a relatively abstract and difficult treatment cast in the language of analytical sociology: it must, nevertheless, be regarded as the basic work for anyone seriously interested in this subject.

Theoretically suggestive and fruitful, albeit incomplete, approaches to understanding the social organization of age can be found in the work of Erik Erikson, *Identity: Youth and Crisis* (Faber, 1968), and in Karl Mannheim's 'The problem of generations', in *Essays on the Sociology of Knowledge* (Routledge & Kegan Paul, 1952). A very convincing presentation of the strengths of longitudinal studies in the study of age is to be found in W. D. Wall and H. L. Williams, *Longitudinal Studies and the Social Sciences* (Heinemann Educational, 1970). And the best discussion of the problems arising in the interpretation of age data in political analysis will be found in David Butler and Donald Stokes, *Political Change in Britain* (Macmillan, 1969).

The HMSO publication, *Social Trends*, should be consulted for up-to-date and fairly straightforward examples of the use of age data to estimate demographic trends and dependency-ratios. Finally, a study which gives a remarkable sense of the extent to which even thet most taken-for-granted attributes of age are in fact socially variable is Philippe Ariès, *Centuries of Childhood* (Knopf, 1960).

Further important references for my chapter are: B. S. Rowntree, *Poverty: a study of town life* (Nelson, 1910); M. Benney, A. P. Gray and R. H. Pear, *How People Vote* (Routledge & Kegan Paul, 1956); B. Bereeson, P. Lazarsfeld and W. McPhee, *Voting* (University of Chicago, 1954); A. Campbell, *et al*, *The American Voter* (New York: Wiley, 1965).

'College generations and their politics', by Seymour Martin Lipset and Everett Carll Ladd Jr appeared in *New Society*, vol. 18 no. 471, 1971.
Philip Abrams

9 Education

I have tried to question several ideas many people have about the role education plays in industrial societies. The first is the relationship between education and economic advancement/economic growth. F. Harrison and C. A. Myers' study of *Education, Manpower and Economic Growth* (McGraw-Hill, 1964) is probably the best single source on the macro-relationship. More recently, R. Hollister, in *Education and the Distribution of Incomes*

(OECD, 1970) has reviewed the literature and recent evidence on personal income and education. The only major British source on this subject is an article ('The economic returns of investment in higher education') in *Economic Trends*, no. 211, 1971.

On the vexed question of education and social mobility, C. Arnold Anderson's article, 'A sceptical note on social mobility', reproduced in A. H. Halsey *et al*, *Education, Economy and Society* (Free Press, 1963) is the most critical introduction.

For an up-to-date account of the impact of educational expansion and changes on inequalities in educational participation, C. Namm, 'Participation and achievement', in *Group Disparities in Education* (OECD, 1971) is comprehensive and thorough. The English classical empirical study on this is J. Floud and A. H. Halsey: *Social Class and Educational Opportunity* (Heinemann, 1957).

Two social studies by F. W. Warburton and V. Southgate: *ITA: an Independant Evaluation* (Murray & Chambers, 1970), and J. Barker Lunn, *Streaming in Primary Schools* (National Federation for Educational Research, 1969), have examined the impact of two major innovations on the educational progress of pupils in British schools. As did an article by myself and colleagues ('Do small classes help a pupil?', *New Society*, vol. 18, No. 473, 1971), these examine the influence of improvements in resource inputs on reading standards. The relative influence of schools and community factors on pupils achievements have been empirically shown in both the Plowden report (Central Advisory Council for Education, *Children and their Primary Schools*), and more recently in G. Peaker's follow-up for the National Foundation for Educational Research *(Plowden Children Four Years Later)*.

Again it is an American source, the Coleman report (US

Department of Health, Education and Welfare, *Equality of Educational Opportunities*, 1964), that provides the most comprehensive analysis of school, home and communal factors on performance.
Alan Little

10 Consumption

This particular chapter could not have been written without the material provided in the Family Expenditure Survey, which is carried out annually for the Department of Employment. Just under 11,000 households are sampled every year, and results not merely are analysed by various classification data, but also compare current findings to those of previous years. The size and complexity of this survey means, in effect, that very few other surveys attempt to cover the same ground.

For the rest, the article depends considerably on reports of market research surveys, primarily concerned with particular subjects. The four which have been most used are as follows: *Patterns in British Holiday Making 1951–1968* (British Travel Association, 1969); *Savings and Investment* (Building Societies Association, 1968); *Choice in Housing* (Institute of Economic Affairs, 1968); *Choice in Welfare* (Institute of Economic Affairs, 1970).

It would have been equally possible to provide similar examples from many other published surveys concerned with specific aspects of welfare, the social sciences, or various commercial products. Much of the data from such surveys has been collated on a regional basis by D. Elliston Allen in his book *British Tastes* (Hutchinson, 1968.) The bibliography for this provides an excellent lead in for surveys on almost all subjects.

Leonard England and Wendy Grosse

11 Nationality and Ethnicity

Excellent, though different, appraisals of ethnicity in the modern world will be found in Philip Mason *Patterns of Dominance* (Oxford University Press, 1970), and Michael Banton, *Race Relations* (Tavistock, 1970). E. Krausz *Ethnic Minorities in Britain* (MacGibbon & Kee, 1971) and E. J. B. Rose, *Colour and Citizenship* (Oxford University Press, 1969) discuss the new salience of 'race' in contemporary Britain. Comparative material is usefully analysed in a special issue of the journal, *Daedalus*, on *Colour and Race* (spring, 1967), and in P. van den Berghe, *Race and Ethnicity* (New York : Basic Books, 1970).

Interesting issues are raised by some chapters contributed by N. F. Bodmer and John Rex in *Race, Culture and Intelligence*, edited by K. Richardson, D. Spears and M. Richards (Penguin, 1972). Important insights on the role of the 'stranger' are still to be found in the writings of Georg Simmel. On what this implies see D. G. Macrae, *Ideology and Society* (Heinemann, 1961), chapter 10, 'Race and sociology', and R. Glass, *Newcomers* (Allen & Unwin, 1960). On 'nationality' and nation-building, and their implications for our time, see R. Bendix, *Nation Building and Citizenship* (New York: Wiley, 1964), and S. P. Huntingdon, *Political Order in Changing Societies* (Yale University Press, 1967). A classic short English work, which much influenced the thinking of Bendix and others, is T. H. Marshall, *Citizenship and Social Class* (Cambridge University Press, 1950).
Julius Gould

12 Religion

These are general discussions of relationships between religion and other variables :

Max Weber's *The Sociology of Religion*, translated by Ephraim Fischoff (Boston, Massachusetts : Beacon Press,

1963), remains essential reading for the breadth of its coverage and the richness of its insight.

Charles Y. Glock and Rodney Stark, *Religion and Society in Tension* (Chicago: Rand McNally, 1965), contains not only some useful analytic discussions, but also presents empirical material on the relationship between religion and politics.

Roland Robertson, *The Sociological Interpretation of Religion* (Oxford: Blackwell, 1970), is mainly analytic work, but it involves summaries of empirical findings – particularly in respect of the issues raised by the Weber thesis concerning the impact of Protestantism. Roland Robertson (ed), *Sociology of Religion* (Penguin, 1969), is a collection of readings drawing on both classical and modern contributions to the problem of the relationship between religion and the wider society.

J. Milton Yinger, *The Scientific Study of Religion* (Collier-Macmillan, 1970), is an extensive discussion, containing many empirical generalisations about the relationship between religion and numerous other variables.

These are studies focusing specifically on religion in relation to clusters of other variables and relying extensively on empirical material:

Robert R. Alford, *Party and Society* (Chicago: Rand McNally, 1963); Nicholas J. Demerath III, *Social Class in American Protestantism* (Chicago: Rand McNally, 1965); S. N. Eisenstadt (ed), *The Protestant Ethic and Modernisation* (New York: Basic Books, 1968); A. M. Greeley, *Religion and Career* (New York: Sheed & Ward, 1963); Gerhard Lenski, *The Religious Factor* (Garden City, New York State: Doubleday Anchor, 1963); Milton Rokeach, 'Value systems in religion', and 'Religious values and social compassion' (*Review of Religious Research*, vol 2, 1970); Richard Rose, *Governing Without Consensus: an Irish perspective* (Faber, 1971); Rodney Stark and Charles Y.

Glock, *American Piety* (Berkeley: University of California Press, 1968).

Other useful contributions are: Michael Argyle, *Religious Behaviour* (Routledge & Kegan Paul, 1958); ITA, *Religion in Britain and Northern Ireland: a survey of popular attitudes* (Independent Television Authority, 1970); David Martin, *A Sociology of English Religion* (Heinemann, 1967); Bryan R. Wilson, *Religion in Secular Society* (Penguin,1969).
Roland Robertson

13 Politics

As will be clear from the chapter, much the most important work on political opinions and voting behaviour in Britain is David Butler and Donald Stokes, *Political Change in Britain* (Macmillan, 1969). Butler and Stokes is important, not merely for the evidence it contains about mass politics, but also for its research methodology and intellectual style. The best general survey of British political sociology – Jean Blondel's *Voters, Parties and Leaders: the social fabric of British politics* (Penguin, 1963) – suffers somewhat from antedating Butler and Stokes, but is still well worth reading.

Among more specialised studies, the following are particularly important: Robert McKenzie and Allan Silver, *Angels in Marble: working class Conservatives in urban England* (Heinemann, 1968) and Eric A. Nordlinger, *The Working Class Tories* (MacGibbon & Kee, 1967), both of which deal with the phenomenon of 'wrong party' voting among manual workers; J. H. Goldthorpe, *et al*, *The Affluent Worker: political attitudes and behaviour* (Cambridge University Press, 1968), which provides additional (and in many ways better) evidence on the same subject, while looking more generally at the political stance of affluent workers; and F. M. Bealey, J. Blondel and W. McCann,

202 *Notes on Further Reading*

Constituency Politics: a study of Newcastle-under-Lyne (Faber, 1965), which is useful in explaining the political sociology and (as it were) the political ecology of a middle-class industrial town.
Anthony King

Some Conclusions

In a sense, further reading for this chapter covers the whole field of sociology. However, students wishing to enter current controversies about the nature and meaning of sociological 'facts' should perhaps start with A. V. Cicourel, *Method and Measurement in Sociology* (The Free Press, 1964); see also Erving Goffman, *The Presentation of Self in Everyday Life* (Penguin, 1971). A classic statement on the assumptions of the empiricists is H. Blumer's article 'Sociological analysis and the "variable"' (*American Sociological Review*, vol. 21, no. 6, 1956). More recently Alan Dawes's pithy piece on 'The two sociologies' (*British Journal of Sociology*, vol. 21, no. 2, 1970) opens up an important issue.

The argument between Runciman and Ingham provides valuable insight into one set of differences: W. G. Runciman, 'Class, status and power?' in J. A. Jackson (ed.) *Sociological Studies I* (Cambridge University Press, 1968); G. K. Ingham 'Social stratification: individual attributes and social relationships' (*Sociology*, vol. 4, no. 1, 1970).

A masterly survey of approaches to the study of social stratification is provided by S. Ossowski in *Class Structure in the Social Consciousness* (Routledge & Kegan Paul, 1963). More recently Frank Parkin has provided a very persuasive analysis of the meaning systems underlying the stratification order in British society which he terms 'dominant' and 'subordinate' (*Class Inequality and Political Order*, Paladin Books, 1972).

Those wishing to pursue the differences between symbolic interactionism and ethnomethodology should look at the reader, *Symbolic Interaction*, edited by J. G. Manis and B. N. Meltzer (Allyn & Bacon, 1967) for the former, and *Recent Sociology*, no. 2, edited by H. P. Dreitzel (Collier-Macmillan, 1970) for the latter. In general, perhaps the two books which reflect current criticism of old-style empirical sociology most effectively are P. Berger and T. Luckmann *The Social Construction of Reality* (Allen Lane, 1967) and A. Gouldner *The Coming Crisis in Western Sociology* (Heinemann, 1971).

R. E. Pahl

Contributors

PAUL BARKER is Editor of *New Society*.

FRANK BECHHOFER is Reader in Sociology, University of Edinburgh.

S. R. PARKER is a sociologist with the Social Survey Division of the Office of Population Censuses and Surveys.

DEREK WRIGHT is Senior Lecturer in Psychology, University of Leicester.

GEOFFREY HAWTHORN is Lecturer in Sociology, Cambridge University.

COLIN BELL is Senior Lecturer in Sociology, University of Essex.
His research assistant, Janet Cabot, also helped with this chapter.

R. E. PAHL is a Professor of Sociology, University of Kent at Canterbury.

MICHAEL CHISHOLM is Professor of Economic and Social Geography, University of Bristol.

PHILIP ABRAMS is Professor of Sociology, University of Durham.

ALAN LITTLE is Director of the Community Relations Commission Research Unit but at the time of writing he was Director of Research, Inner London Education Authority, and Visiting Professor, University of Surrey. (The opinions in his article are his, not those of the ILEA.)

LEONARD ENGLAND and WENDY GROSSE are directors of the market research firm of England, Grosse & Associates.

JULIUS GOULD is Professor of Sociology, University of Nottingham

ROLAND ROBERTSON is Professor of Sociology, University of York.

ANTHONY KING is Professor of Government, University of Essex.